The NEW RIBBON EMBROIDERY

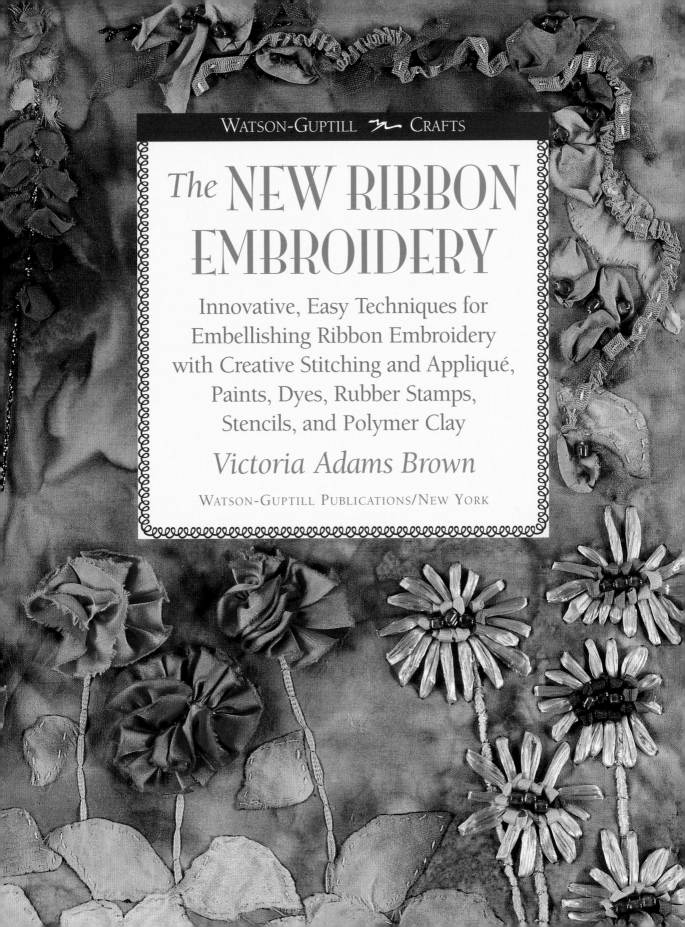

WATSON-GUPTILL ～ CRAFTS

The NEW RIBBON EMBROIDERY

Innovative, Easy Techniques for
Embellishing Ribbon Embroidery
with Creative Stitching and Appliqué,
Paints, Dyes, Rubber Stamps,
Stencils, and Polymer Clay

Victoria Adams Brown

WATSON-GUPTILL PUBLICATIONS/NEW YORK

TO J.M., O.B., Q.B., L.L., AND RAYMOND

Notes on the Art

On the front cover: The fabric ground is watercolored silk charmeuse. The fish appliqués are made from bias-cut silk and Ultrasuede and embellished with sequins and Delica seed beads. Tiny fish stenciled with Lumiere paint "float" at the top of the composition. The fish and seahorse fins are made from bias-cut silk. The pods in the bottom lefthand corner are made from vintage velvet remnants. Vintage 1920s gold netting fills the bottom of the design. Amethyst, quartz crystal, and rose quartz stones are embroidered among a sea bed of Delica seed beads, vintage puffed silver balls, and nylon cording. Sea ferns stitched with green variegated 4mm Heirloom Sylk ribbon and feather stitching in metallic threads complete the design.

On pages 2–3: The composition is stitched on a cotton fabric printed with a silk-painted and salted pattern. Appliquéd pieces of burned silk, raffia, bias-cut silk ribbons, Mokuba organdy ribbon, and assorted fibers provide dimension and a range of textures.

Senior Editor: Candace Raney
Edited by Joy Aquilino
Designed by Areta Buk
Graphic production by Ellen Greene

First published in 1997 by Watson-Guptill Publications,
a division of BPI Communications, Inc.,
1515 Broadway, New York, N.Y. 10036

Library of Congress Cataloging-in-Publication Data
Brown, Victoria Adams.
    The new ribbon embroidery: innovative, easy techniques for embellishing ribbon embroidery with creative stitching and appliqué, paints, dyes, rubber stamps, stencils, and polymer clay/Victoria Adams Brown.
        p. cm. — (Watson-Guptill crafts)
    Includes index.
    ISBN 0-8230-3171-3
    1. Silk ribbon embroidery.   I. Title.   II. Series.
TT778.S64B764   1997
746.44—dc21   97-19403
                                                        CIP

Manufactured in Hong Kong

First printing, 1997

1 2 3 4 5 6 7 8 9 / 05 04 03 02 01 00 99 98 97

Also by Victoria Adams Brown
From Watson-Guptill Publications

The Complete Guide to Silk Ribbon Embroidery: Basic, Step-by-Step Techniques for Making Beautiful Designs for Wearables, Accessories, and Home Decor

If you would like to contact Vickie Brown, please write to her at the following address:
Shrieking Tree Farm
P.O. Box 416
Fountainville, Pennsylvania 18923
E-mail: 102515,3570@Compuserve.com

ACKNOWLEDGMENTS

I would like to extend my gratitude to several individuals who contributed to the fulfillment of this project.

At Watson-Guptill Publications, senior editor Candace Raney granted me the perfect vehicle for sharing my concept of ribbon embroidery and mixed media by encouraging me to write this book. Developmental editor Joy Aquilino imposed a consistent rhythm on the text and images, and designer Areta Buk once again masterfully arranged all the elements to create a beautiful book.

The following women—all true visionaries—were exceedingly gracious in sharing their ideas with me while I assembled the manuscript. I would like to express my appreciation to surface designer Patsy Moreland, for sharing her friendship and wealth of knowledge. My thanks also to Susan Kocsis at Rupert, Gibbon & Spider, for her generosity in providing products for use in the demonstrations; and to Michelle Hester at Silkpaint Corporation, for the support she extended through her innovative product lines and numerous brainstorming, "what if" phone sessions.

Photographer Susan Alderfer used her talent and skill to document my work through her camera lens. We became quite the team: As I photo-styled hundreds of setup shots in my barn studio, Sue determined the most complementary angle and lighting.

While I designed, dyed, painted, sketched, stitched, and wrote, I had one constant companion who kept "animal hours" with me and provided levity when humor was scarce. Although her stitching skills are lacking—furry, six-toed paws can be something of a hindrance in executing any stitch—her passion for silk ribbons is equal to my own: As I stitch with them, she sleeps among them. Her antics gave me laughter and patience during many long, isolated days of focus and intensity. Her delightful spirit motivated me to write a children's book, which now resides in my computer awaiting my illustrations of a beribboned yellow cat. Olive, thank you for your presence. Girlie, the Tuna Treat's on me!

After enduring the process of assembling a book twice, my husband Michael, my dream financier and a true gentleman, has more than a mere working knowledge of silk ribbon embroidery. His patience and tolerance inspire me daily, and I am indeed in debt to his gracious spirit.

CONTENTS

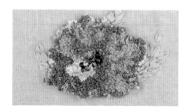

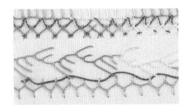

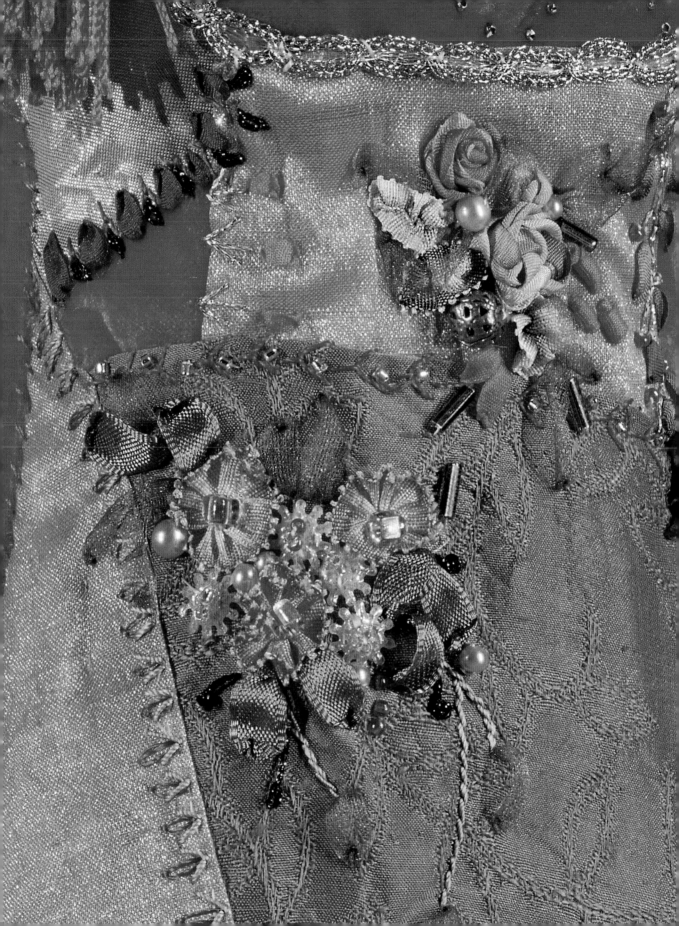

INTRODUCTION

While working on *The Complete Guide to Silk Ribbon Embroidery* (Watson-Guptill Publications, 1996), I began visualizing the myriad possibilities that could be achieved by exploring ribbon embroidery along with a variety of popular craft media. I imagined that interest in ribbon embroidery could be expanded by providing an accessible survey of several creative paths that could be traveled either one at a time or simultaneously to create unique projects.

The results of those thoughts and ideas are presented in *The New Ribbon Embroidery*. In some instances, I investigated a topic simply because I knew that information about it couldn't be found anywhere else, or that what was available was limited in scope. So that readers can attempt to paint and dye ribbon, thread, and yarn with confidence, I've included an in-depth chapter that describes a range of products and techniques. In addition, there are chapters on how to combine basic embroidery stitches, ribbon manipulation techniques such as folding and gathering, and an assortment of beads and trimmings to create vibrant animal and floral motifs. These motifs can be further embellished with crazy quilt stitches and appliqué methods, which are also reviewed. A chapter on working with craft media surveys stamping, stenciling, watercolor, silk painting, and polymer clay. To provide inspiration and to teach by example, the final chapter scrutinizes the process of blending and juxtaposing ribbon embroidery with various craft media by describing the development of nine original and diverse projects. A source directory has been added to ease readers' frustrations in finding the tools and materials that are used throughout.

The New Ribbon Embroidery is intended for a broad audience: For quilters, dollmakers, miniaturists, knitters, and crocheters who simply want to enhance their designs with silk ribbon embroidery, or who want to take embellishment to new heights; for stitchers who are looking for imaginative ideas on how to recycle fabrics and give new life to old garments; for rubber stamping, stenciling, watercolor, and polymer clay enthusiasts who want to apply their craft to new surfaces; for fabric and silk painters who want to incorporate silk ribbon into their projects; for ribbonwork designers who want to paint and dye their own ribbons; and for fiber artists whose love of textiles motivates them to explore new creative territory.

I hope that this book meets the expectations set by its title: To give readers a first-hand view of how to create beautiful gifts and keepsakes by using ribbon embroidery and other craft media in new and resourceful ways. Enjoy!

A detail of the crazy-quilted dress form project (see page 131).

EMBELLISHING SILK RIBBON

(Opposite) A silk handbag featuring folded silk-satin ribbon roses embellished with the pan-painting technique (see page 34). (Right) Wire-edge and silk ribbons painted with Pébéo Setasilk silk paints (see page 23).

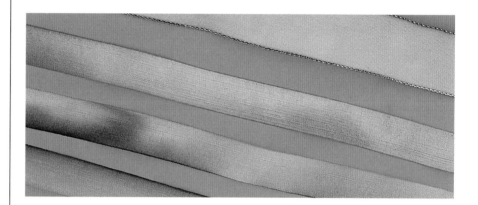

This chapter surveys easy techniques for handpainting and hand-dyeing a wide range of ribbon widths and fibers—including bias-cut silk, velvet, organdy, wire-edge, and synthetic—and even thread and wool, all with strikingly beautiful results. Methods for cutting bias-cut ribbon from undyed silk fabric and recycled silk garments are demonstrated. The differences between paints and dyes and their effects on various fibers are reviewed, as are the topics of preparing ribbons for dyeing and painting as well as gathering and organizing essential tools and supplies. Painted and dyed ribbons can be further embellished by applying salt or alcohol while they are still wet, or by burning their edges into unusual shapes after they have dried.

Rather than presenting a set of hard-and-fast rules, this chapter should serve as a jumping-off point for exploring remarkable ribbon color and surface design, while easing the apprehension that often comes with trying something new.

CREATING ONE-OF-A-KIND RIBBONS

Upon seeing a display of silk ribbon in a craft or sewing store, crafters and stitchers who are new to ribbon embroidery may think that every color of the rainbow can be found among those shelves. After stitching with purchased silk ribbons for some time, I realized that due to space limitations my local retail sources could offer only the most widely used colors, which meant that my palette was pretty much limited to pastels.

I then began adding variegated and ombré silk ribbons to my stitch designs. Variegated ribbons are ribbons that have been hand-dyed with two or more colors; ombré ribbons are dyed with several values of a single color. Both types of ribbon can be used to stitch multicolor motifs, but instead of having to stop each time to re-thread the needle with a different color of ribbon, just one ribbon will do the job. Unfortunately, both variegated and ombré ribbons can be difficult to find in retail stores, so they usually must be obtained through mail-order sources.

Eventually, I realized that the best way to expand my creative options was to paint and/or dye white (undyed, unbleached) ribbon myself. By using a variety of readily available fabric paints and dyes, I could produce virtually any color or color combination, in any width or fiber of ribbon, custom-made for each particular design. I also found that I could paint and variegate my purchased ribbons, thereby making the most of the ribbon inventory I already had on hand.

In addition to creative flexibility, I was able to reap other benefits from this sudden insight. First and foremost was my cost savings, since I would no longer have to purchase several colors in set amounts of yardage. I could also save time and energy on looking for sources whose variegated and ombré ribbons met my projects' requirements. I could custom-design and stitch a gift for a friend or loved one featuring his or her favorite colors. By keeping accurate records of how I dyed and painted my ribbons I could duplicate colors consistently, or I could choose to experiment and explore without the pressure of having to document every color combination. Having the freedom to create your own ribbons not only expands your creative horizons, it's also a lot of fun.

As time passed, handpainting and -dyeing ribbons became just as addictive as stitching with them, and ultimately led me to explore the possibility of incorporating variations in texture into my stitch designs by painting and dyeing bias-cut silk (see page 14), organdy, velvet, synthetic, and wire-edge ribbons, as well as wool yarn and a variety of threads. That experimentation in turn prompted me to combine various dyeing and painting techniques, to produce unusual effects by applying salt and alcohol to wet dyes and paints, and to invent unique freeform shapes by burning the edges of dyed and painted ribbons. All of these simple techniques are summarized and demonstrated in this chapter.

Spools of white, undyed ribbon and buttonhole twist thread. From left to right: Petersham, organza, velvet, 32mm, synthetic 4mm, 7mm silk, 13mm silk, silk-satin, synthetic wire-edge, and a card of silk buttonhole twist thread. Ribbons by Ribbon Connections.

BIAS-CUT SILK RIBBON

Bias-cut silk ribbon's method of fabrication and unusual physical properties make it a unique embroidery element. Bias-cut ribbon is made by cutting silk yardage at a 45-degree angle to its weave, creating an unsealed edge that will fray slightly during stitching but won't unravel completely. The fraying of bias-cut ribbon is further enhanced when it is pulled through tightly woven fabric. This vintage effect looks especially attractive on floral motifs.

Undyed silk bias-cut ribbon, which is made from white flat crepe, charmeuse, or jacquard silk, can be purchased in 1/4-inch (0.64-cm) to 2-inch (5-cm) widths, in 5- to 25-yard (4.5- to 22.5-m) rolls. I prefer to work with flat crepe silk, which is very smooth and drapes gracefully with gentle ripples. Though it has a tendency to wrinkle, it irons easily with a warm iron. When dyed, this silk fabric exhibits a beautiful sheen.

Before dyeing or painting purchased 2-inch-wide (5-cm-wide) silk bias-cut ribbon, cut the diagonal seams that run throughout the roll off of each length of ribbon. After the ribbon has been dyed or painted, you can then cut it into the widths you need for your stitching project. I generally cut widths of approximately 7mm (1/4 inch) and 13mm (1/2 inch), which I thread on #16 or #18 chenille needles. The 7mm width is the narrowest recommended width, since the ribbon frays on both edges. When stitching with bias-cut ribbon, always use short lengths of approximately 7 inches (17.8 cm). Longer lengths of bias-cut ribbon, which are subject to stress as they are pulled through fabric—sometimes causing the ribbon to break—can be used to make gathered flowers (see pages 82–84).

I prefer to create my own bias-cut ribbon. Cutting bias-cut ribbon is fun and easy, offering stitchers a new direction in which to develop their silk ribbon embroidery. Cutting the ribbon yourself takes just a few minutes and is economical compared with purchasing a roll of bias-cut silk. You can begin by working with undyed white silk fabric, but if you have a silk garment that you can't wear anymore because it's stained, or if you find an old silk blouse in a thrift shop, you can recycle it by cutting it into bias ribbons and use them to enhance a new garment or other project.

Before bias-cutting white, undyed silk fabric, preshrink it by handwashing it with a gentle detergent and letting it air-dry. If you're cutting up a recycled silk garment, it's likely that the garment was shrunk when its fabric was dyed; if you have any doubts, wash the garment as described above before cutting it. You can then cut fabric squares out of the garment and use them to create bias-cut ribbon in a variety widths.

I find that the cutting process is easiest when using a cutting mat called Strips Ahoy, which is equipped with a plastic slotted grid that is closed over the fabric to hold it in place as it is cut with a rotary cutter. The slots, which are spaced at 1/2-inch (1.3-cm) intervals, are used as guides for positioning the rotary cutter.

Take the bottom lefthand corner of a silk square and fold it over to meet the top righthand corner. Place the folded fabric on the cutting mat and align the fold with one of the vertical slots in the plastic sheet. Close the plastic sheet over the fabric, insert the blade of the rotary cutter at the top of one of the slots, then pull the cutter toward you. As you cut the fabric, do not roll the cutter back and forth in the slot, and do not take it out of the slot. If the fabric has not been cut completely, insert the rotary cutter blade at the top of the same slot and pull it toward you once more.

Bias-cut silk ribbons can be dry cleaned or gently washed by hand and allowed to air dry. Because of the ribbon's frayed edges, wearables and other items embellished with bias-cut ribbon should not be put in the washing machine or dryer.

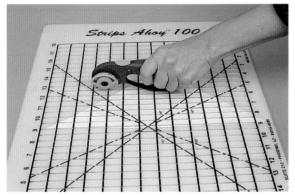

Using a Strips Ahoy cutting mat and plastic grid to cut a folded square of silk on the bias with a rotary cutter.

Bias-cut silk ribbons.

A simple gathered rose and leaves made with purchased 2-inch-wide (5-cm-wide) bias-cut flat crepe silk. Note the luster and sheen of the ribbon and its slightly frayed edges.

WOOL EMBROIDERY

Offering stitchers yet another creative option, wool yarn simultaneously complements and provides an attractive contrast for silk and other ribbons. By using the same embroidery stitches, these two textures can be combined to create elegant compositions.

To stitch the sample shown below, I used a three-ply 100-percent virgin Persian lamb's wool yarn that was developed for museum-quality work and is used primarily for needlepoint and other fine embroidery techniques. This yarn, which is available from It's Polite to Point (see source directory), is made in 500 colors. Note that good-quality wool yarn can be dyed using any of the techniques demonstrated in this chapter.

A gathered silk ribbon rosette (see page 84) and cascading Japanese ribbon stitches and French knots are surrounded by a variety of embroidery stitches stitched with one ply of wool yarn on a cinnamon velvet ground.

WORKING WITH DYES AND PAINTS

This chapter offers stitchers and crafters simple, easy methods for dyeing and painting white undyed ribbon as well as colored ribbon, thread, and yarn in all types of fibers. The dyeing techniques illustrated in this chapter are overdyeing, tea dyeing, dyeing in a plastic bag, immersion dyeing, dip dyeing, and variegating; the painting techniques covered are fan-brush painting, misting, pan painting, space painting, and edge painting. Before you begin—even before you start experimenting with ribbons you have on hand—you should be aware of the important differences between the working characteristics of fabric dyes and paints (see "Dyes and Paints," page 21).

To prepare ribbons and fabrics for dyeing or painting, soak them in a cool bath of water for 1 to 2 minutes, then remove them and allow them to air-dry. This step not only prevents shrinkage the first time you wash them but removes sizing and other chemicals so that the fibers can accept paints and dyes more readily. Once ribbons have dried, cut their ends on the diagonal to prevent unraveling.

ESSENTIAL SUPPLIES

The basic supplies needed for dyeing and painting ribbons are easy to find and relatively inexpensive. You may even have some of them on hand. Note that once you've used any of the following items with paints or dyes, you should permanently relegate them to your craft studio and never use them to prepare or serve food.

Organizing Your Workspace. Before you begin, you should prepare yourself for—and protect your worksurface from—those inevitable spills and drips.

- *Plastic cover or tablecloth.* Cover your worksurface with plastic before painting or dyeing ribbons. Some fabric dyes can stain permanently; once they've dried, fabric paints can become difficult to remove without damaging a surface.
- *Paper towels.* These are used primarily for wiping up spills and spots, but their absorbency can be exploited in other ways. For example, paper towels can be used to blot ribbons that have been overly saturated with dye or paint, or as a surface for drying wet ribbons when pastel effects are desired.
- *White plastic-coated freezer paper.* This nonabsorbent surface, which is coated with plastic instead of wax, can be used to keep ribbons in place during the painting process (see "Preparing Ribbons for Painting," page 30) and for drying wet ribbons. Unlike paper towels, freezer paper will not affect the intensity of dyed or painted ribbon because it won't absorb any moisture or color. A small piece of freezer paper can also be used as a temporary palette for fabric paints.

Mixing and Organizing Dyes and Paints. You should have access to several sizes and types of containers for holding and measuring dyes and paints.

- *Infant bathtub.* You'll need one of these if you plan to immersion-dye garments, yardage, or large amounts of ribbon.
- *Measuring cups or beakers.* You can use either glass or plastic containers for measuring dye ingredients, but glass is preferable to plastic because it won't stain. Plastic containers often stain after only a single use, making it impossible to evaluate the color of a dye mixture accurately. If possible, buy measuring cups marked with both U.S. and metric measurements.
- *Clear plastic cups.* These disposable cups can be used to mix and hold small batches of dye or paint.
- *Plastic 6-well paint tray palettes.* These are perfect for holding tiny amounts of paint and dye.
- *White Styrofoam plates.* Disposable plates made from nonabsorbent materials can serve as palettes for paints.
- *Glass eye droppers.* These are used to mix precise dye and paint colors, by carefully blending two colors one drop at a time, and to apply dyes, paints, and alcohol to ribbon and fabric. Most dyers and painters find it's best to have at least six on hand.
- *Ribbon graspers or holders.* A wide range of household items can be used to remove ribbons from a dyebath, or move them from one dyebath to another, while keeping fingers dry. Try any one of the following and see which works best for you: hair wave clips, kitchen tongs, long tweezers, or binder clips. Hemostats (see page 45) can also be used for this purpose, but they are somewhat expensive.

Brushes and Other Applicators. There are several choices available, depending on your personal preference and the desired effect:

- *Fabric paint brushes.* These brushes are designed specifically for use with acrylic fabric paints, but can also be used with dyes. Their stiff bristles are best suited for controlled applications.
- *Chinese calligraphy brushes.* The hairs of these inexpensive brushes form a nice sharp point. They can be used to apply either dyes or paints.
- *Fan brushes.* As their name implies, the hairs in these brushes are arranged in a fan shape. Great for making squiggles and wavy lines, they can be used to apply either dyes or paints.
- *Foam brushes and brayers.* These highly absorbent brushes, which are generally 1 inch (2.5 cm) wide, are used to apply generous amounts of dye or paint to fabric or ribbon. They can also be used to create wet-on-wet effects by saturating fibers with water before applying dye or paint, so that colors will bleed and run together, for a loose, painterly look.
- *Cotton swabs.* Though their capacity for making precise renderings is somewhat limited, dual-end cotton swabs are an inexpensive substitute for brushes that can be used with either dyes or paints.

What to Wear. It's just as important to protect yourself from splashes and smudges as it is your workspace. Make sure you won't mind if the clothes you're wearing become stained with dye or splotched with paint. Old clothes used for yardwork or housework are best. Also, have ready access to lots of cold water and plastic containers for rinsing.

- *Fitted plastic disposable gloves.* Although I generally wear these only when working with dyes, they're recommended for people whose skin is sensitive to paint ingredients or to prolonged exposure to water. If you don't wear gloves when working with dyes, you will surely end up with stained fingers and hands.

- *Hand cleaner.* If I get a tear in the fingers of one of my gloves during a dyeing session and can't remove the stains with regular soap and water, I use ReDuRan, a hand cleaner designed specifically to remove dye stains (distributed by Rupert, Gibbon & Spider). This type of cleaner is abrasive, so it should be used sparingly. Read the manufacturer's label instructions before using.

- *Hand lotion.* Because silk and other delicate fabrics can snag on rough hands, I use hand lotion to combat dry skin. The lotion I have found to be the best—and I've tried them all—is "The Hoofmaker" by Straight Arrow, which is made for conditioning horses' hooves. It is inexpensive, greaseless, absorbs immediately, and won't stain fabric. This lotion can be purchased at any farm supply store and at many mass merchant locations.

Some of the items used when dyeing and painting ribbons and fabrics.

KEEPING A RIBBON JOURNAL

Before you begin a painting or dyeing session, you should consider starting a ribbon journal. This type of project diary is fun to keep and requires minimal effort.

I began keeping a journal after a few frustrating instances of trying to reconstruct how I had achieved a specific color or effect during a previous session. Now, I create a page in my journal for each project, noting the date, the type of ribbon, the brand(s) of dye and/or paint I'm working with, the formulation of the paint mixture or dyebath, the technique used to create the color or effect, and the weather conditions (whether humid or dry, as this affects the performance of dyes and paints). I usually include personal notes about the project I was designing and the activities taking place in my studio that day. Then I attach sample ribbon swatches to the page, place the page in a protective plastic sheet, and store the sheet in a three-ring binder.

Of course, since a journal is a very personal document created specifically for one individual's use and enjoyment, some of what I feel is important enough to record may not be of interest to others. I'm always glad that I've taken the time to catalog the results of my creative experimentation. That way, I have all my formulations at my fingertips, I can enhance colors or develop new techniques based on my initial notes, or I can share my painting and dyeing "secrets" with friends.

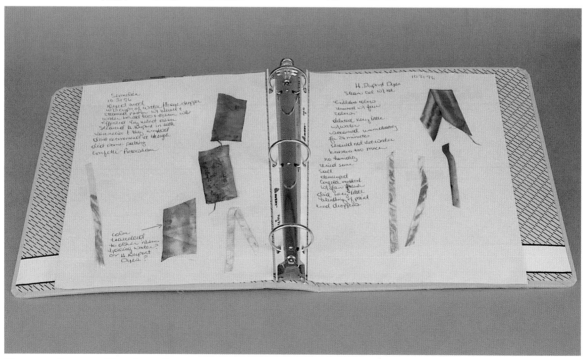

Two pages from my ribbon journal.

DYES AND PAINTS

Fabric dyes and paints can both be used to add color to ribbons and threads, but the effects they produce are completely different. Because these media often have misleading brand names—paints are sometimes called dyes, and vice versa, and both are often vaguely referred to as "colors"—it is particularly important to understand the differences between the two.

Since most fabric paints simply coat fibers with a layer of opaque or semiopaque color, leaving behind a slight stiffness or "feel," the results of applying fabric paints are the same regardless of a ribbon's width or type of fiber.

In contrast, dyed color bonds with fibers, creating a subtle sheen and softness that cannot be achieved with paints. Because of this, the character of the ribbon, thread, or yarn fibers significantly affects the final look of the medium. For example, since organdy is sheer, dyed colors appear translucent and pale, while on velvet, which is dense, colors look richer and more intense. Synthetic ribbon—both standard and wire-edge—dyes well, although the colors are somewhat muted compared to silk. The colors of purchased, already dyed ribbons can also be enhanced with dyes, for example, by striping, overdyeing, or variegating, with the original color of the ribbon affecting the final results.

Of course, your personal color preferences will also figure largely in the equation. Since I enjoy using a vibrant and varied palette, I like to paint or dye most of my ribbons with several colors. Some stitchers prefer a more subtle look, and thus use fewer or less intense colors, or both.

The products described below were chosen based on a few simple criteria: ease of use, availability, and breadth of application. Note that most of the paints and dyes must be set with heat, either dry or steam (see "Drying and Setting Methods," page 38).

DYES

Rit Tint & Dye and Dylon Cold Water Fabric Dye. These products, which can be used with cotton, rayon, linen, silk, wool, and polyester/cotton blends, are both excellent for dyeing large amounts of ribbon (as much as 1 pound or 3 yards [0.45 kg or 2.7 m] of fabric). They are particularly well-suited to dyeing items that will be repeatedly machine washed. To use, simply follow the package instructions. The entire process takes less than an hour—simply place wet ribbon or fabric in the dyebath and stir for 5 minutes, let stand for 50 minutes, then rinse in tepid water—and no heat-setting is required.

Jacquard Procion MX Fiber-Reactive Dyes. This product, which is manufactured by Rupert, Gibbon & Spider, is concentrated dye that yields brilliant, permanent color. Procion dye is also very economical: 1 ounce (31 grams) of powder can dye up to 5 yards (4.5 m) of fabric. It performs extremely well with a range of fibers, including silk, wool, rayon, velvet, cotton, linen, and even hemp, flax, and wood. Rinse the fabric in a solution of Synthrapol (a mild soap) and water; set aside. Fill a 5-gallon (19-l) plastic bucket with 3 gallons (11.4 l) of hot water. Add salt and dye as directed; when dissolved completely, add the wet fabric and stir constantly for 20 minutes. Dissolve soda ash in 1 quart (0.93 l) of hot water, then add to the dyebath (but do not pour it directly on the fabric). Stir the dyebath every 5 minutes for a total of 50 minutes. Remove the fabric from the dyebath and rinse it in cold water. To set and remove excess dye, wash the fabric in a mixture of 3 gallons (11.4 l) of hot water and 1½ teaspoons (7 grams) of Synthrapol. Rinse, then let air dry.

Tinfix, Super Tinfix, and Peintex Dyes. All of these professional-grade products are manufactured in France by Sennelier and can be found in art supply stores or purchased through mail order. Peintex is a water-based ink dye that can be used with all fibers except wool. Its clean, dazzling colors, which leave ribbons soft, are heat-set with an iron. Tinfix and Super Tinfix dyes, which also create brilliant colors, can only be used with silk and wool and must be heat-set with steam.

ColorHue Instant-Set Dyes. This product, which can be mail-ordered directly from Things Japanese (see source directory), can only be used with silk. ColorHue dyes are highly concentrated; to achieve a medium value, mix 1 teaspoon (5 grams) of dye mixed with ½ cup (120 ml) cold water. When immersion-dyeing (see page 24), stir the dyebath continuously and let soak for a few minutes. After dyeing, immerse ribbons in water to remove any residual dye, then dry and heat-set damp ribbons by ironing them with a dry iron set on the "cotton" setting.

Jacquard Silk Colors. Available by mail order and at many art supply stores, these dyes are made exclusively for use with silk. They are nontoxic, odorless, and lightfast, and can be either handwashed or dry cleaned. Once dry, set dyes by immersing ribbon or fabric in a solution of Jacquard Permanent Dye Set Concentrate and cold water; stir for 5 minutes, then rinse. These dyes can also be heat-set with steam.

H. Dupont Dyes. These silk-only dyes are available in a range of radiant colors and are set with steam. Distributed by Silkpaint Corporation, Inc., H. Dupont dyes can be found in most art supply stores or ordered by mail.

PAINTS

In contrast to dyes, whose applications are sometimes limited to specific fibers, most fabric paints can be applied to any type of fabric surface. The paints listed below are all nontoxic, available in a range of colors, and can be found in most craft and hobby stores. Note that craft-grade acrylic paints can also be used to paint ribbons and fabrics.

DecoArt So-Soft Fabric Acrylics. This line of fabric paints can be thinned with water, does not require heat setting, and remains soft after it's dried.

Delta Starlite Dye Shimmering Fabric Colors. Because these paints are too thick to be used straight from the bottle, they must be mixed with a 1:1 solution of distilled water and vinegar; this step also ensures that ribbons remain soft and stitchable after drying and heat-setting. This brand of fabric paints, which contain small metallic flecks that yield a pearlized surface finish, looks particularly attractive on silk-satin ribbon. Heat-set ribbons by ironing them on the reverse side. Do not wash ribbons or fabric for at least one week after painting.

Elegance Fabric Dyes. These fabric paints from Koh-I-Noor are stronger and more vivid in color than most other brands. Thinning these paints with water causes the pigment to separate from the vehicle as it dries; this may be desirable for a contemporary look, but to avoid this effect, dilute them instead with Koh-I-Noor fabric paint extender. To give these paints an iridescent sheen, mix them with Koh-I-Noor fabric paint pearlizer. Heat-set after drying; do not wash ribbons for one week after painting.

Jacquard Dye-na-Flow. Manufactured by Rupert, Gibbon & Spider, this line of highly concentrated fabric paints is made to simulate dyes. These extremely versatile paints can be used with cotton, silk, and synthetic fabrics, and are the only brand of fabric paint that works with salt applications (page 36). Once dry, these paints must be heat-set, either with an iron or by placing them in a clothes dryer for 20 minutes on the "damp dry" setting.

DekaSilk. These intensely colored paints from Deka work well on cotton, silk, and synthetic fabrics. Like Dye-na-Flow paints (see above), they can be thinned with water, and are heat-set either in a clothes dryer or with an iron.

Pēbēo Setasilk. These fabric paints, which are designed exclusively for use with silk, can be thinned with either water or extender. Once dry, these paints remain soft and are heat-set with an iron.

Lumiere Metallic Fabric Paints. Made by Rupert, Gibbon & Spider, Lumiere is a metallic fabric paint that dries quickly and without stiffening fibers. Lumiere is available in gold, bronze, pearl, and silver. It requires no heat-setting.

A selection of fabric paints and dyes: Delta Starlite Dye Shimmering Fabric Color; Jacquard Dye-na-Flow by Rupert, Gibbon & Spider; H. Dupont Dye by Silkpaint Corporation; Super Tinfix by Sennelier; Rit Tint and Dye; Dylon Cold Water Dye by Prim-Dritz; ColorHue Instant-Set Dye by Things Japanese; Tinfix by Sennelier; Elegance Fabric Dye by Koh-I-Noor; Lumiere Metallic Fabric Paint by Rupert, Gibbon & Spider; DecoArt So-Soft Fabric Acrylic; DekaSilk; Pēbēo Setasilk; and Jacquard Silk Color.

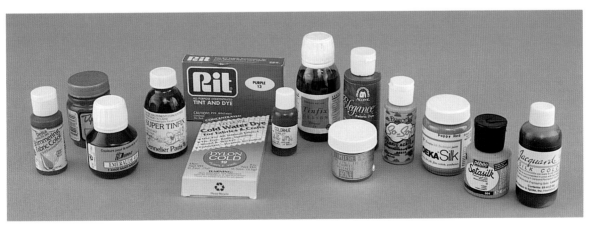

DYEING TECHNIQUES

All of the techniques described below involve immersing ribbons, yarn, or thread in a dyebath, either partially or completely. Dyes can also be applied to ribbons using any of the painting techniques discussed on pages 31–35.

IMMERSION DYEING

The following is a basic method for immersion dyeing, in which a relatively large item such as a garment or silk yardage or a large amount of ribbon is dyed in one single color. Dylon, Rit, and Procion dyes are most appropriate for this technique. (Of course, small amounts of ribbon can be immersion-dyed in small dyebaths.) The instructions below apply to Rit and Dylon dyes only; the instructions for using Procion dye are on pages 21–22.

1. Presoak the item or items in a mild solution of soap and water, then rinse. Fill an infant bathtub or other large container with enough water to immerse the item. Prepare the dye solution according to package directions, pour it into the tub, then stir the dyebath with a wooden spoon.

2. Immerse the item completely in the dyebath, stir for 10 minutes, then let stand for 50 minutes. Remove the item from the dyebath, rinse it in cool water, then hang to dry.

3. An inexpensive silk champagne-color silk chemise purchased for several dollars at a local thrift store immersion-dyed with Dylon Cold Water Fabric Dye in rose violet.

1

2

3

TEA DYEING

In addition to commercially manufactured dyes, tea can be used to immersion-dye ribbons and fabrics to achieve an aged or vintage look. Tea will dye or stain a variety of fabrics, but natural fibers are generally more receptive and thus dye more deeply, while synthetic fibers usually tea-dye to just a pale tint.

Steep several bags of regular tea in boiling water for 5 to 6 minutes. When the tea reaches the desired color, pour it into a container and place the ribbon or fabric in it, immersing it completely. To impart a rich, warm glow to white ribbon or fabric, let stand for 15 minutes, then remove from the tea. For deeper, richer shades, let stand for several hours or overnight. Once the fabric has reached the desired shade, rinse it in cold water and let air-dry. No heat-setting is required.

Rit makes a dye that duplicates the effects of traditional tea dyeing, but the intensity of the color is based on the formulation of the dyebath and the amount of ribbon or fabric that's being dyed, rather than the duration of the immersion. The Rit tea dye is somewhat gentler on silk fibers, and works best on cotton, rayon, linen, and blends of these; wire-edge ribbons, 100-percent polyester or acrylic fabrics, and fabrics with special finishes are not recommended for use with this product.

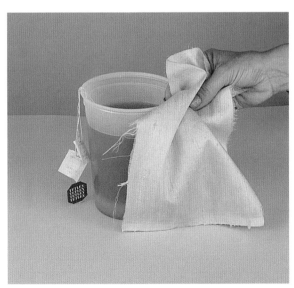

After immersing it in tea for 15 minutes, this piece of dupionni silk obtained a subtle golden warmth.

This piece of silk, which was left in tea overnight, has a stronger, richer color.

OVERDYEING

Overdyeing involves immersion-dyeing ribbons that have been previously painted or dyed. In fact, any of the painting and dyeing techniques described in this book—for example, space painting, edge painting, misting—and even fabrics texturized with salt or alcohol can be further enhanced with immersion dyeing.

Because overdyeing will substantially and irrevocably affect the hues, intensities, and values of already painted or dyed ribbons, it is recommended that you test-dye small pieces of ribbon before committing an entire batch to a dyebath.

The color of the spatters on these misted ribbons darkened considerably after overdyeing.

OMBRÉ AND VARIEGATED RIBBONS

To create basic ombré ribbons, you will need four plastic disposable cups, a glass eye dropper, and several hair wave clips, binder clips, or other tools for grasping and holding ribbons. Pour a 1/2 cup (120 ml) of water into each of the four cups. Prepare the dye solution as directed on the package instructions, then use the eye dropper to place 6 drops of dye into the first cup, 12 drops of dye into the second cup, 18 drops of dye into the third cup, and 24 drops of dye into the fourth cup. Attach a hair wave clip to a ribbon, then submerge the entire length of ribbon into the first cup for about 15 minutes. Remove the ribbon from the first cup, then place about three-quarters of its length into the second cup for the same length of time. Repeat, placing half of the ribbon into the third cup, then a quarter of the ribbon into the fourth cup. Allow the ribbon to air dry on freezer paper, then heat-set as directed.

Immersion times and dyebath formulations may differ, depending on the dye that is used. To create variegated ribbons, mix a different color for each cup, or use more than four cups. You can also use an eye dropper to mix special shades by gradually adding one or more dye colors to another.

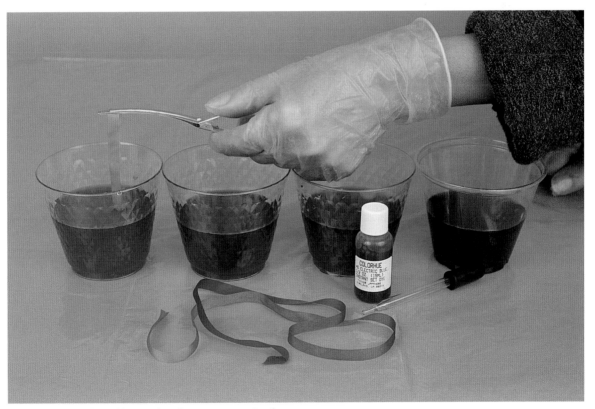

Creating blue ombré ribbon with ColorHue Instant-Set dye.

DIP DYEING

Dip dyeing is an easy way to create variegated and ombré wool yarn. Fill three disposable plastic cups with about a ½ cup (120 ml) of water each. Prepare the dye solutions as directed, use an eye dropper to add about 10 drops of dye into each cup, then stir each dyebath with a straw or coffee stirrer. (Use a separate eye dropper and stirrer for each color.) Take approximately 1 yard (0.9 m) of yarn and place a portion of it into each cup. The dyes will be absorbed by and migrate through the strands of wool, automatically variegating the yarn. When the desired color has been achieved, remove the yarn from the dyebaths and rinse it in cold water until the water runs clear. Let air-dry, then heat-set as directed.

Although this dyeing technique can also be used with ribbons, note that each color of dye will only affect the portion of ribbon that is immersed in it; the dyes will not migrate through the fibers and variegate the ribbon as they do in yarn.

A yard of wool yarn is distributed among three Peintex dye colors.

Dip-dyed variegated yarn. The colors are light because the yarn was left in the dyebaths for only a few minutes. For darker colors, leave the yarn in the dyebaths for longer intervals.

DYEING IN A PLASTIC BAG

By crowding several items into a plastic bag containing a small amount of dye so that none of the items is saturated with color, a "batik" or mottled look can be achieved. For this technique, you'll need a quart-size (0.95-l) heavy-duty plastic freezer bag, 1 cup (240 ml) of prepared dye, and enough fabric or ribbon to fill the bag. (Make sure the fabric and dye are compatible.) Pour the dye into the bag, then place the items inside the bag. If you're dyeing fabric, fold it so it fits snugly in the bag; if you're also dyeing ribbon or yarn, place them in the inner folds of the fabric. (When dyeing small amounts of ribbon or yarn, use less dye and a smaller plastic bag.) None of the items should be completely immersed in dye. Seal the bag, set it upright on a flat surface, and let stand for a few minutes. To create the mottled effect, reposition the bag every few minutes, first on one side, then on the other.

Once the desired shade has been reached, remove the items from the plastic bag, rinse them in a plastic bowl of cool water, let air dry, then heat-set according to the package instructions. If the colors of the ribbon or yarn are not dark or intense enough, pour some of the dyebath into small plastic cups, wrap each individual length of ribbon or yarn around a plastic straw, and dip the straws into the dye. Agitate and keep turning the straws so that each end will come in contact with the dye; do not submerge the straws completely.

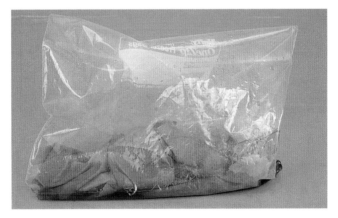

Fabric, ribbon, and yarn are crowded into a resealable plastic bag with a small amount of burgundy Rit dye.

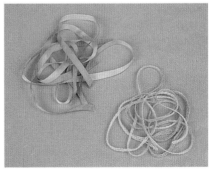

After a short interval, a subtle mottling was achieved on both the cotton muslin fabric (left) and the ribbons and yarn (right).

PAINTING TECHNIQUES

In this book, the term "painting technique" is defined as a method in which either dye or paint is applied to ribbon with a brush or other applicator. If you've decided to color ribbons in this manner, chances are you'll want to control the results, at least to some extent. Silk embroidery ribbons are in their most fragile state when wet, their fibers stretched and swollen with moisture. When ribbons are painted in close proximity, they somehow tend to gravitate toward one another, sometimes creating a tangled mess. Therefore, unless you're aiming for an entirely spontaneous effect, it's essential that ribbons be prepared before painting so that they stay in place and their colors remain distinct, both during the painting process and as they air-dry.

PREPARING RIBBONS FOR PAINTING

Painting Dry Ribbon on Freezer Paper. Lay several unpainted ribbons on an ironing board. Take a sheet of freezer paper and lay it, slick side down, on top of the ribbons. Using an iron set on a dry-heat setting, iron the freezer paper. This adheres the ribbons to the paper, keeping them manageable during the painting process. Once the ribbons have been painted, they can air-dry (and, in some cases, be heat-set) directly on the freezer paper. If you transfer the ribbon to dry on paper towels, the toweling will absorb much of the color.

Painting Stretched Ribbon, Wet or Dry. This technique is especially effective when painting large quantities of ribbon. To stretch ribbon, you will need two shoebox bottoms, two bricks, and two binder clips. Place a brick in each one of the shoebox bottoms, then clip an end of ribbon to each box. Pull the boxes apart to stretch the ribbon until it is taut. The ribbon can then be painted dry; for more spontaneous "wet-on-wet" effects, saturate the ribbon first by applying clear water with a foam brush or cotton swab. If you're working wet-on-wet, don't be alarmed if the ribbon stretches and sags a little. Allow the ribbon to air-dry in the stretched position, then heat-set following the manufacturer's instructions.

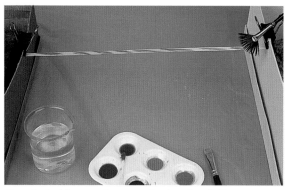 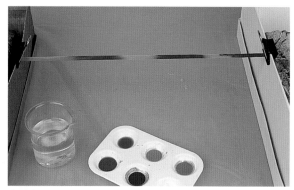

Stretched ribbon can be painted either dry (left) or wet-on-wet (right).

FAN-BRUSH PAINTING

This is an extremely simple painting method. Iron the ribbon onto freezer paper or stretch it as described above. Load a fan brush by swishing its bristles through dye or paint, even out the load and remove any globs by working the hairs on a separate surface, then use a zigzag motion to apply the medium to the entire length of ribbon. When the ribbons are stitched, the dye or paint will appear as small flecks of color.

You can use a fan brush to apply dyes and paints in a variety of other ways. See also "Space Painting," page 33.

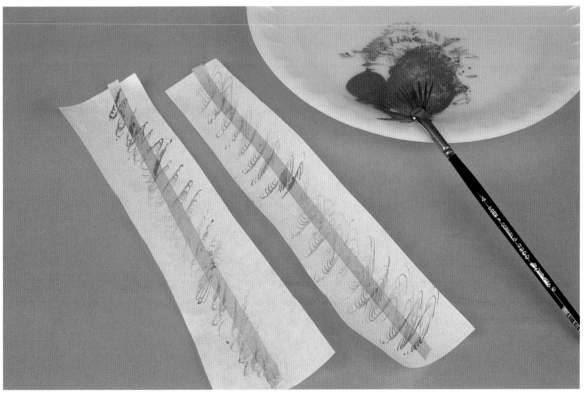

Ribbon painted with the fan-brush technique.

EDGE PAINTING

Edge painting is a wet-on-wet technique; the ribbon is wet down with water before dye or paint is applied so that the colors will flow together and intermingle. Iron the ribbon onto freezer paper as described above. Use a foam brush or cotton swab to wet the entire ribbon with water, but do not allow the water to puddle on the ribbon. Load a ¼-inch-wide (0.64-cm-wide) fabric paint brush or foam brush with dye or paint, then paint the freezer paper immediately next to the edge of the wet ribbon. The dye or paint will flow through the water and onto the edge of the ribbon, then slowly migrate toward the middle. Repeat on the other side of the ribbon, either with the same or another color. If the ribbon is wide enough, you can paint a stripe down its center, either with a mixture of the two edge colors or with a third color. Let the ribbon dry directly on the freezer paper, then heat-set as directed.

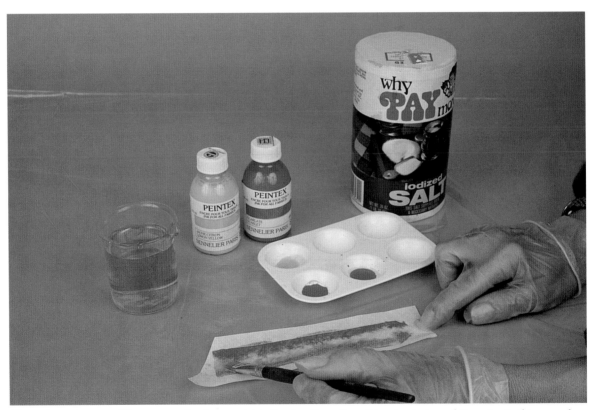

The moisture in a wet ribbon attracts the dye or paint to its edge, then allows it to migrate toward its center. In this example, Peintex dyes in lemon yellow and scarlet were mixed to create an orange hue, then the orange was applied to one edge and the scarlet to the other, and the yellow was painted down its center.

SPACE PAINTING

Space painting is an easy way to produce variegated or ombré ribbons. The final effect is more random than any of the preceding painting techniques, so the methods of preparing ribbons for painting by either ironing them to freezer-paper or stretching them between two weighted shoeboxes do not apply here.

Cover a small piece of cardboard with plastic wrap and secure it with double-sided masking tape. As a rule of thumb, you should use a 2- × 5-inch (5- × 12.7-cm) piece of cardboard to space-paint 2 yards (1.8 m) of ribbon; use larger pieces for longer lengths of ribbon. Place a piece of double-sided masking tape at each end of the cardboard, then wind the ribbon around the cardboard, making sure the entire width of the ribbon is exposed. Paints or dyes can be applied to either dry or lightly moistened ribbon.

For variegated ribbon, assemble two or three colors of dye or paint, then apply each one to approximately one-third of the wrapped ribbon with a Chinese calligraphy or fabric painting brush. Turn the cardboard over and repeat. Note that variegated ribbon produced by space-painting is more varied in appearance than that made by the dyeing technique described on page 27.

For confetti ribbon, wrap the ribbon around the cardboard as described above, lightly load a fan brush with dye or paint, and apply it to the ribbon in a zigzag motion as described under "Fan-Brush Painting" (see page 31). Apply two more colors in the same manner, then repeat on the other side of the cardboard.

Once both sides of the wrapped cardboard have been painted, let the dye or paint set for a few minutes, gently pull the ribbon off the cardboard, let air-dry on a hanging rack, then heat-set according to the manufacturer's instructions.

1. Cover a piece of cardboard with plastic wrap, place a piece of double-sided masking tape at either end of the cardboard, then wind the ribbon around it.

2. To yield a spontaneous effect, the ribbon was first moistened with a foam brush, then water-thinned Jacquard Dye-na-Flow paints were applied with a Chinese calligraphy brush.

3. Dyed variegated ribbon.

4. The space-painting technique can also be used to create confetti ribbons. In this example, undiluted Dye-na-Flow paints were applied with a fan brush in a zigzag pattern to dry Petersham ribbon (a type of grosgrain ribbon).

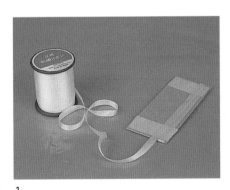

1

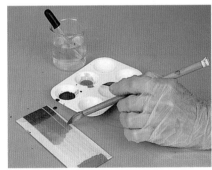

2

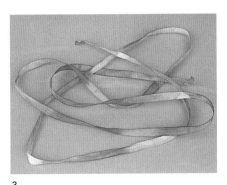

3

4

PAN PAINTING

This easy wet-on-wet painting technique yields the most spontaneous and painterly effects. Like space painting, pan painting eliminates the need to prepare ribbons by stretching them or ironing them to freezer paper.

Simply moisten a length of ribbon with a foam brush and place it in a foil pie pan. Using a separate brush for each color, randomly paint it with several shades of dye or paint. Because the ribbon is wet, the colors will flow into each other. Transfer the ribbon to a piece of freezer paper and let air-dry, then heat-set according to the manufacturer's instructions.

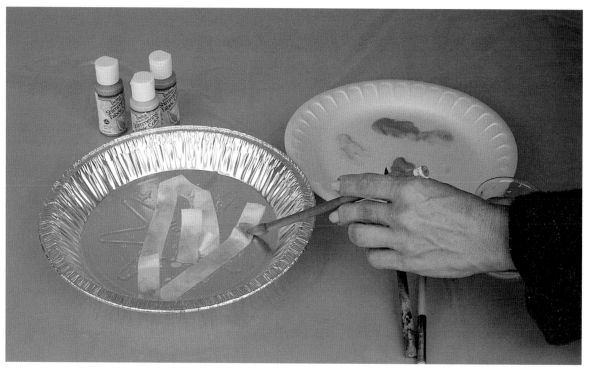

Pan-painting silk-satin ribbon with several colors of Delta Starlite Dye Shimmering Fabric paints. Their colors dry to a shimmering pale finish enhanced by the luster of the silk-satin ribbon. See page 10 for a finished example.

MISTING

This painting method is different from the others in this book in that it uses a plastic spray bottle instead of a brush to apply paint or dye. Note that commercially dyed ribbons do not readily accept misted dyes and paints. Experiment with a few different brands of dye or paint to see which yield the best results.

Iron several ribbons to a piece of freezer paper as described on page 30, then attach the freezer paper to a rigid surface that can be propped upright. (I tape the freezer paper to a plastic box lid, which I then stand on a small easel.) Fill a small plastic spray bottle with dye or thinned fabric paint; the paint must be thin enough to be pumped through the nozzle, but should not be so diluted that its color looks anemic. Test the spray on another surface before spraying the ribbons. Holding the bottle approximately 8 inches (20.3 cm) away from the ribbons, spray them with short, quick bursts of color. When you've finished misting, place the freezer paper on a flat surface and allow the ribbons to air-dry. Heat-set according to the manufacturer's instructions.

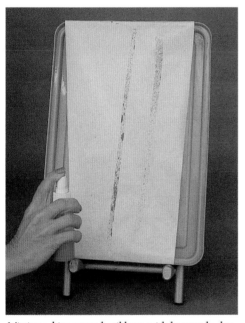

Misting white organdy ribbons with burgundy dye.

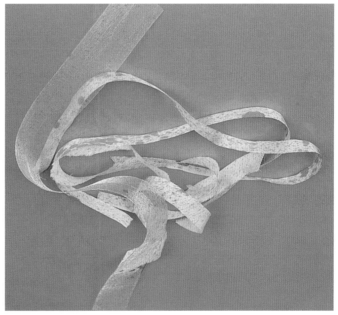

Dried, misted ribbons.

SALT AND ALCOHOL EFFECTS

A variety of unusual textures and effects can be created by applying salt or alcohol to ribbons and fabrics while dyes and paints are still wet.

SALT

When applied to dyed or painted ribbon while it is still wet, grains of salt produce small dark flecks and draw colors in various directions. A range of results can be achieved, depending on the type of salt that is used. Regular table salt, flake salt, and rock salt can all be used for this purpose. Simply sprinkle a small amount of salt onto the wet ribbon, let the dye or paint dry completely, then gently brush away the salt.

Salt effects are particularly impressive on bias-cut silk ribbon. I like to dye, then salt 2-inch-wide (5-cm-wide) bias-cut silk ribbon, let it dry, then cut small strips from it with my rotary cutter. When used for stitching, these ribbons are unique and dazzling.

Note that low humidity is best for creating salt effects; high humidity can prevent them from occurring. Also, salt reacts best with silk-only dyes applied to silk ribbon, and the only brand of fabric paint that responds to salt is Jacquard Dye-na-Flow (see page 22).

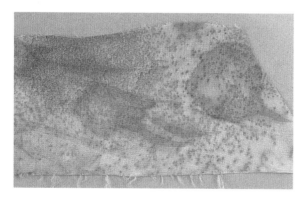
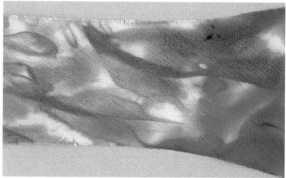

Salt effects produced on H. Dupont dyes using table salt (above left), rock salt (above right), and flake salt (right).

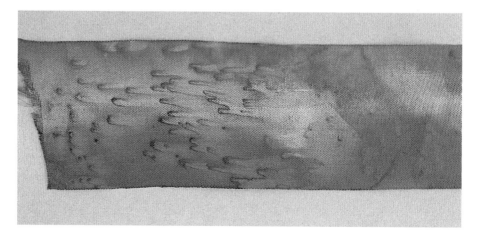

ALCOHOL

For a more dramatic effect, fill an eye dropper with isopropyl alcohol and slowly release a drop onto wet dyed or painted ribbon. A light circle will form and gradually enlarge as the dye moves away from the alcohol. Other applicators, such as a cotton swab, a brush, or a plastic spray bottle, can also be used to apply alcohol.

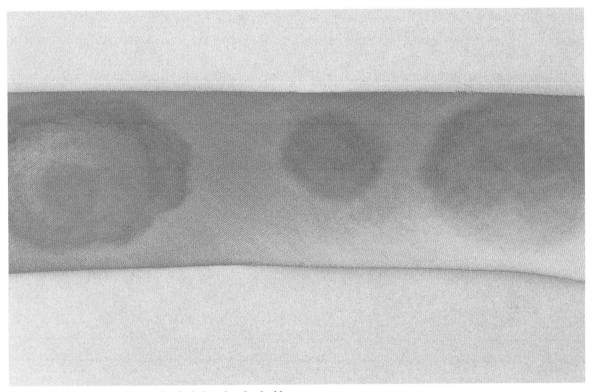

An eye dropper was used to apply alcohol to this dyed ribbon.

DRYING AND SETTING METHODS

AIR-DRYING DYED AND PAINTED RIBBON

There are several ways to air-dry dyed or painted ribbons. After removing immersion-dyed ribbons from a dye bath, you can lay them on a piece of freezer paper, wax paper, or plastic wrap, or hang them on a collapsible hanging rack. If you use a rack, place a plastic dropcloth underneath it to catch any drips. Make sure to clean the clamps from time to time, or dye from previous batches of ribbon may be transferred to the latest batch.

If you prepared your painted ribbons by stretching them or ironing them onto freezer paper, you can simply let them air-dry just as they are. A rack is an ideal place to dry painted ribbons, as it takes up very little space and allows ribbons to dry more quickly. Note that a few droplets of dye or paint may accumulate on the ends of the ribbon and drip off onto the dropcloth.

Whether ribbons are dyed or painted, avoid using paper towels as a drying surface. Because paper towels are so absorbent they soak up much of the color, leaving dried ribbons pale. In most instances, the colors of wet ribbons are significantly brighter and more saturated than they are after they've dried, even without blotting them on an absorbent surface.

A collapsible hanging rack can be used to air-dry dyed and painted ribbons.

HEAT-SETTING DYES AND PAINTS

Depending on the manufacturer's instructions for each individual brand of dye or paint, color is usually set, or made permanent, by applying heat, either dry or wet. Dry heat is most typically applied with an iron, but a hair dryer or clothes dryer can sometimes also be used. Wet heat is administered with the simple method of steam-setting described on page 40.

Setting with Dry Heat. In most cases, the term "heat-setting" indicates that the dye or paint is set with an iron set on the "cotton" setting.

Ribbons that have air-dried on freezer paper should be placed on the ironing board with the ribbons beneath the paper and the dull side of the paper facing up. Before you start, protect the ironing board from stray or still-damp dye or paint by covering it with a press cloth or towel. Using a dry iron set on the "silk" setting, iron the paper very quickly—just to a count of three—then lift the paper away from the ironing board and remove the ribbons from the paper.

A professional press-style iron, such as an Elna Press Mini Tailor, can provide a fast and easy way to heat-set dyed and painted ribbons. Set the press on the "silk" setting, lightly mist the ribbons with water, lay a press cloth or towel on the ironing surface, then position the ribbons on the iron and cover them with another press cloth. Close the top of the press, hold the handle in place for a few seconds, then open it. The ribbons are dry, flat, and ready for stitching.

A batch of damp ribbons that has all been dyed or painted with just one color can be heat-set by placing it in a lingerie bag or an old sock and drying it in the clothes dryer on the "fluff" or "air only" setting for 20 minutes.

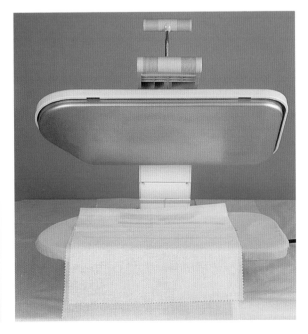

Either a traditional iron or a professional press such as this one can be used to heat-set dyes and paints with dry heat.

Setting with Steam. Deterred by the cost of professional steamers and the amount of time the steaming process requires, some consumers avoid using dyes and paints that are set with steam heat, which also produces the deepest and most vibrant colors. With these consumers in mind, I developed an easy method for steam-setting silk ribbon that yields intense color.

Since dyes and paints should not be used in a kitchen or steam-set on a kitchen stove, you'll need to create your steaming setup in a sewing room or craft studio, using a hot plate that can heat water to a boil. Place 1¼ inches (3.2 cm) of water in the bottom of a large stainless-steel stock pot and bring it to a boil. Once the water reaches a boil, reduce the heat to medium so that the water remains at a gentle simmer. NOTE: It is absolutely critical that the water *not* boil while ribbons are being steam-set; should it reach a boil, the water will splash onto the ribbons, causing the colors to migrate and run, ruining the entire batch.

Place a steaming net over the lip of the pot, put the air-dried dyed or painted ribbons into the net, then place a folded white bath towel over the pot. Cover the pot with its lid, place another white bath towel on top of it, then set a brick on top of the towel. After steaming the ribbons for exactly 26 minutes (time them with an egg timer), remove the brick, pot lid, and towels and place the ribbons in a metal strainer. Rinse the ribbons with cold water until the water runs clear, then air-dry them on a rack.

When steam-setting, make sure the water is at a gentle simmer before placing the ribbons into the steaming net. Steaming nets available from Silkpaint Corp.

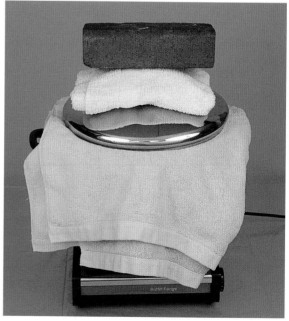

Cover the top of the net with a white bath towel, place the lid on the pot, then place another towel and a brick on top of the lid. Steam the ribbons for 26 minutes, remove them from the net, rinse with cold water, then let air-dry.

BURNING RIBBON

Once their colors have been heat-set, dyed and painted natural-fiber ribbons can be burned into unusual shapes. This method, which can yield unexpected and dramatic results, is typically used to prepare embellished ribbon for appliqué (see pages 100 and 128).

Using sharp scissors, cut out some shapes from dyed or painted silk or cotton ribbon (I like to make freeform leaves). Fill a measuring cup about halfway with water and set it in the center of a foil pie pan. Place a dripless candle into the cup, then light the candle. Holding a cut ribbon shape with both hands, "dip" the edges of the shape into the side of the flame and burn them to a dark charcoal color. The longer the piece is held into the flame, the more dramatic the final shape will be; if you want to retain the shape of the cut ribbon, pass its edges through the flame fairly quickly. (Cotton ribbon will have a wider burned edge.) Place the burned ribbon on a paper towel and gently remove the charred edges. They will flake off easily, leaving the ribbon edge smooth but dark.

Note that synthetic fibers react somewhat differently to heat. In most cases, the edges of synthetic ribbons will clump and bead rather than burn; in others, the fibers are so heat-sensitive that the ribbon will curl and turn under without actually touching the flame.

1

2

3

1. Pass the edges of the cut ribbon through the side of the flame.

2. Flake off the charred edges over a piece of paper toweling.

3. Six pieces of burned silk ribbon, ready for appliqué.

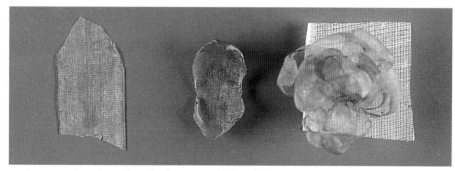

In this example, a 3/4-inch-wide (1.9-cm-wide) hand-dyed synthetic organdy ribbon was cut into 1 1/4-inch (3.2-cm) strips, then the ends of each strip were cut into points. When exposed to the flame, the ribbon curled up; there was no charred residue to remove. Several curled strips were then stitched together to make a small flower.

EMBROIDERY BASICS

(Opposite) Blue columbines with twisted Japanese ribbon stitches (see page 49) in 4mm lavender silk ribbon. (Right) A detail of an elaborate freeform flower stitched with punch needle embroidery (see page 58).

The material requirements for a silk-embroidered project are fairly simple, but before you begin your silk ribbon odyssey you should understand the elements of the craft. Most of the items discussed in this chapter can be purchased at fabric, craft, and hobby stores. If you can't find a local retail source for your supplies, or if you can't find something that's used in one of the projects in this book, consult the source directory (page 142).

This chapter also reviews the basic handling requirements and working properties of silk ribbon, including the procedure used to thread a needle. In addition, this chapter demonstrates fourteen simple stitches, many of which are basic embroidery stitches that have been used for hundreds of years.

GETTING READY TO STITCH

A conveniently packaged assortment of embroidery needles.

There are a few topics that must be addressed in order to prepare for stitching with silk ribbon. In addition to a review of basic tools and stitching aids, you should understand the fundamentals of handling ribbon.

ESSENTIAL TOOLS

Needles. I believe I have found the best ribbon embroidery needle assortment pack on the market—it meets all my stitching needs. Made in England by Prym-Dritz, this 13-needle assortment includes beading needles, standard embroidery needles, and a #16 needle (absolutely essential for stitching with wide ribbons). The pack is especially convenient when traveling.

Scissors. A pair of small embroidery scissors with sharp blades is an indispensable stitching tool. To avoid stressing or fraying the ends of your ribbons with anything less than clean, sharply made cuts, buy the most expensive scissors your budget will allow, and use them *only* to cut ribbon or fabric. Maintain the blades' sharpness by honing them on a sharpening stone.

Embroidery Hoops and Q-Snaps. Whenever possible, you should mount your project on an embroidery hoop. A hoop holds fabric taut and flat so that your fingers are free to manipulate the ribbon, and keeps the rest of the fabric from interfering with your stitching.

I prefer to use good-quality wooden German hoops that are specifically designed for machine embroidery. These hoops will last a lifetime, and their hardwood frames will never form rough edges that can snag ribbon or fabric. Because they are thinner than regular hoops they are excellent for ribbon embroidery, making it easier for the stitcher to reach the center of the fabric. A 3- to 5-inch (7.6- to 12.7-cm) circumference is recommended, with a 4-inch (10-cm) circumference allowing for the most efficient manipulation of the ribbon. The tension in a wooden hoop is adjusted by turning the screws on the upper stave. Wooden hoops can be purchased at most craft and fabric stores.

Designed to prevent the wrinkling that often occurs with a wooden hoop, a Q-Snap consists of a rectangular plastic frame that supports the fabric from below, and four plastic sleeves that clip onto the frame over the fabric to keep it in place. The tension is adjusted by shifting the sleeves with a flick of the wrist. The entire assembly quickly snaps apart for easy transport. Available in a variety of sizes, a large Q-Snap is particularly useful for stitching large-scale projects, as it provides a generous view of the stitching surface. Q-Snaps are generally found in smaller sewing and quilting shops.

Of course, there are some projects for which a hoop is not appropriate, such as hats, small areas of garments like lapels and collars, and delicate, lightweight silks, which could become stretched or misshapen. If you must work lightweight silk on a hoop, wrap the staves with yarn or surgical tape.

Hemostats. When working with 13mm (¹/₂-inch), 32mm (1¹/₄-inch), and even wider or heavier ribbons, I use either hemostats or round-nose pliers to pull them through fabric. Hemostats, which are normally used during surgery to compress bleeding blood vessels, can be purchased at medical and nursing supply stores. They are somewhat expensive, but they can be used for a wide range of craft tasks (see page 18). Round-nose pliers can be purchased at most craft and bead stores. Simply bring the tip of the needle through to the front of the fabric, and grasp the barrel of the needle with the hemostat or pliers, and pull the needle and ribbon through the fabric.

Hand-eze Craft Glove. Embroidery can place undue strain on hands and wrists, especially when working with hemostats or pliers (see above). Craft gloves can be particularly effective in reducing hand stress common to needlework. Hand-eze, a therapeutic craft glove developed by a New England research group, provides relief from a variety of continuous-motion hand and wrist disorders, including fatigue, arthritis, tendonitis, and carpal tunnel syndrome. Available at most craft, hobby, and fabric stores, Hand-eze gloves can also be used while performing other repetitive manual tasks.

Nymo Beading Thread. Available at most bead stores and through mail order (see source directory), Nymo beading thread is an extremely strong nylon thread made in two weights, "O" and "D." Since its filaments aren't twisted, it is very easy to thread. I generally use the "O" weight, which comes in fifteen colors. I use the taupe or champagne thread for a variety of stitching tasks, including beading, couching, tacking, and gathering ribbon. Because this neutral color is practically invisible, it saves time spent re-threading needles with different colors of floss.

Delica Beads. Delica beads are used to embellish many of the samples and projects in this book, as their "flash" and sparkle enhance any stitch design.

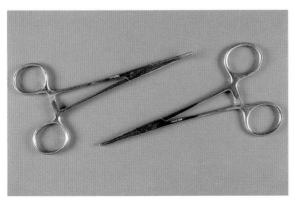

Hemostats are great for pulling wide and heavy ribbons through fabric.

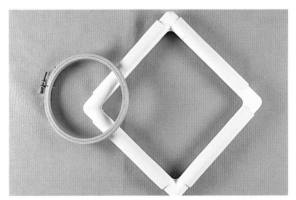

A 4-inch (10-cm) embroidery hoop and an 8-inch (20.3-cm) Q-Snap.

Manufactured in Japan by Miyuki Shoji Co., Ltd., Delica beads can be found in bead shops and purchased by mail (see source directory). Often called "antique" or "delicious" beads, these cylinder-shaped beads have polished ends and thin walls with large, easy-to-thread holes. They are made in 300 colors (most stores usually carry around 100), and are packaged in 5-gram (0.2-ounce) tubes that contain about 1,000 beads.

E6000 Adhesive. This product is an industrial-strength permanent glue and sealant that provides superior adhesion on wood, metal, ceramic, glass, and plastics. Although its adhesive bond sets within 10 minutes, it requires 24 hours to cure completely.

Fray Check. A clear, quick-drying liquid seam sealant, Fray Check is applied to ribbon ends and to the cut edges of fabrics that have a tendency to ravel to prevent fraying. Machine-washable and dry-cleanable, Fray Check is recommended for finishing the ribbon stitches on all wearables. Silk and synthetic ribbon are both prone to slipping, making it easy for ends to come loose, especially on garments that are worn often.

WORKING WITH PATTERNS

To create patterns for the animal motifs shown on pages 62–73, use a pencil or black fineline marker to trace the outlines of the motif's elements onto a sheet of tracing paper, then enlarge or reduce the tracing to the desired size on a photocopier. Use the tulle netting transfer method to transfer the motif to fabric: Lay a piece of tulle netting over the traced pattern, then trace it onto the netting with a permanent black fineline marker. Pin the netting to the fabric, then use a water-soluble marking pen to outline the pattern. Remove the netting and begin stitching. When the stitching is complete, remove any visible marks with a damp cloth or cotton swab.

For simple marking tasks, you'll want to use a fade-away pen. These pens are best suited to simple projects that can be completed in one sitting. Depending on the fabric, a design can last up to several hours before the purple ink fades away. (Note that fade-away pens are generally not suitable for use with damasks, as the ink tends to vanish within minutes.) Any marks that remain after stitching can be removed with a damp cloth or cotton swab.

WORKING WITH SILK RIBBON

To control silk ribbon's natural tendency to twist and curl, you should thread the needle with 12 to 14 inches (30.5 to 35.6 cm) of ribbon, a length that can be maneuvered with little difficulty. As you gain experience and skill, you can try working with 16 inches (40.6 cm) of ribbon, which will allow you to make several stitches before having to re-thread the needle. (Use shorter lengths when working with wider widths of ribbon.) The technique you use to thread the needle will depend on the width of the ribbon you're working with. See "Threading and Locking the Ribbon," page 47.

Occasionally, when a length of ribbon is too long, the weave of fabric too tight, or the fashioning of a stitch distorted, silk ribbon (and, less frequently, synthetic ribbon) can *fray*. This undesirable phenomenon is different from the feathered edges that can be produced on bias-cut silk ribbon (see page 14). On 4mm ribbon, fraying appears as small loops or picots along the edges; on 7mm and wider ribbons, the fibers separate, or *stripe*, creating an unsightly stress line down the middle. Both of these problems make stitchwork look worn and tired. If your ribbon begins to fray, remove the stitches and discard the frayed ribbon, then re-thread the needle with a shorter length.

Manipulating the Ribbon. While most of the stitches used in this book require that the ribbon remain flat or untwisted, you'll probably only need to use your thumbs and index fingers to ensure that it remains straight as you work. Use the thumb of the hand in which you're grasping the hoop to hold the ribbon flat against the fabric. Then, as you pull the needle back through the fabric, tighten the ribbon over your thumb to ensure its smoothness. When the ribbon becomes twisted, use a *laying tool* to fix it. You can use practically anything as a laying tool—the eye end of a large, blunt needle, a toothpick, or even the needlework tool specifically manufactured for this purpose—as long as it accomplishes the objective: to eliminate the twists and curls on the front of the fabric so that subsequent stitches are uniform and attractive. Insert the laying tool into the loop of the ribbon and pull the ribbon up through the fabric several times. The twists in the ribbon will ease out as the ribbon slides over the tool. Once the twists have been removed, you can complete the stitch.

Threading and Locking the Ribbon. When threading a needle with 4mm silk ribbon, the ribbon is locked into the eye of the needle. Locking this width of ribbon into the eye prevents it from slipping out of the needle, so that the ribbon has to be cut out of the eye when the stitches are completed. In contrast, 7mm ribbon and wider ribbons are simply inserted through the needle's eye and left unknotted; if these ribbons were locked, the act of pulling them through the fabric would cause them to stripe. Regardless of width, always cut the ribbon at a 45-degree angle for easy insertion into the eye. Leave a 1/2- to 1-inch (1.3- to 2.5-cm) tail on the back of the fabric with the first stitch, then anchor it in place with the next stitch.

1. Pull approximately 3 inches (7.6 cm) of 4mm ribbon through the eye of the needle, then pierce it about 1/2 inch (1.3 cm) from the end.

2. Gently pull the long tail of the ribbon until the pierced piece locks over the eye of the needle.

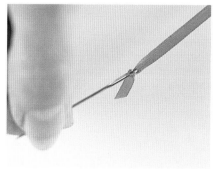

1

2

BASIC EMBROIDERY STITCHES

STRAIGHT STITCH AND WHIP STITCH

The straight stitch is the most elementary of all flat stitches. It can be used singly to create a small bud, overlapped in a circle to make a rose, or "wrapped" with ribbon with to make a whip stitch.

1. Come up at point A and go down at point B, making sure that the ribbon isn't twisted. The stitch should lie flat on the surface of the fabric when the ribbon is pulled through.

2. A completed straight stitch. The look of the stitch will vary according to the degree of tension used to pull the ribbon through the fabric. If a whip stitch is desired, proceed to step 3.

3. Slide the needle underneath the straight stitch, taking care not to snag the ribbon or pierce the fabric. Keeping the ribbon smooth and flat and using consistent tension, loosely wrap the stitch with the ribbon two or three times.

4. After completing the final wrap, bring the needle through the fabric on the side of the wrapped stitch.

5. A completed whip stitch. By increasing the tension on the ribbon when ending the stitch, the stitch can be curved slightly, producing a curved whip stitch.

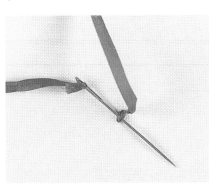

1

2

3

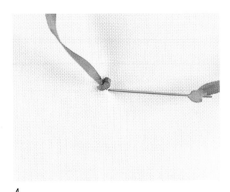

4

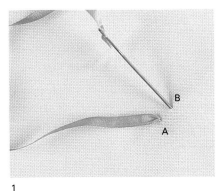

5

JAPANESE RIBBON STITCH

The Japanese ribbon stitch is extremely versatile. Not only is it possible to vary the lengths of the stitches and the degree of tension used, but stitches can also be layered using two widths of ribbon.

If all your attempts at Japanese ribbon stitches somehow turn into straight stitches, slow down! You're probably pulling the ribbon through the fabric too quickly, thus preventing the small curl at the end of the stitch from forming.

1. Come up through the fabric at point A. Untwist the ribbon so that it lies flat on the fabric. Insert the needle into the center of the ribbon approximately ¹/₄ inch (0.6 cm) away from point A.

2. To form the curl of the completed stitch, pull the needle through the ribbon slowly and gently.

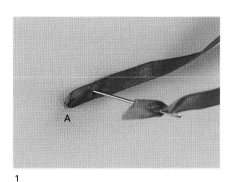

1

2

TWISTED JAPANESE RIBBON STITCH

This stitch is similar to the Japanese ribbon stitch, except that the ribbon is twisted before it is pierced with the needle.

1. Bring the needle and ribbon through the face of the fabric. Twist the ribbon loosely either once or several times, depending on the desired effect.

2. Pierce the ribbon with the needle, pulling it slowly through the fabric to create a curl at the end of the stitch.

3. A completed twisted Japanese ribbon stitch.

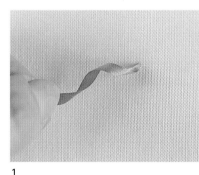

1

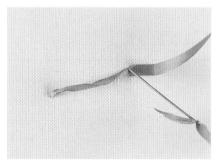

2

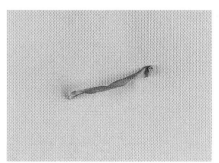

3

SATIN STITCH

Essentially a series of parallel, side-by-side straight stitches, the satin stitch can cover large areas quickly. Use it to fill in shapes, such as an animal's body, a landscape element like a path or a lake, or a large bow on a baby blanket.

1. To make a single satin stitch, simply come up at A and go down at B.

2. Repeat step 1 to lay a second satin stitch directly beside the first.

3. Continue adding stitches until the shape has been filled in.

1

2

3

COUCHING

Another type of flat stitch, the couching stitch is very old and extremely easy to execute. I usually use couching to attach braiding, vintage metal threads, and other materials that are not suitable for stitching. If you want to make sure that your couching is perfectly straight, lightly draw a straight line on the fabric with a water-soluble marking pen, position the ribbon or thread over the line, then begin couching. Couching is also a good ornamental appliqué stitch (see page 70 for an example).

1. Position a piece of ribbon or thread on the surface of the fabric, or stitch a long flat stitch (straight or Japanese ribbon) by coming up at A and going down at B. Using ribbon or thread in a contrasting or complementary color, come up through the fabric at C (near either A or B).

2. Go back down at D while holding the ribbon or thread in place. Repeat steps 1 and 2 at regular intervals along its entire length.

3. A 4mm pink silk ribbon couched with purple metallic braid.

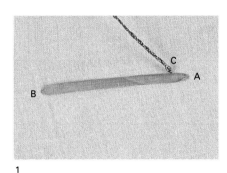

1

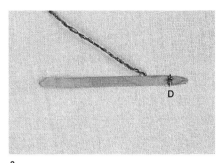

2

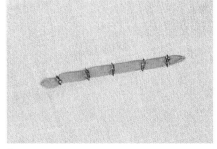

3

LATTICE COUCHING

Lattice couching is a composite stitch consisting of straight and cross stitches. Long, widely spaced, parallel straight stitches are stitched first in one direction, then overlapped with another set of straight stitches positioned perpendicular to the first set to create a grid. The grid is then couched with cross stitches where the long straight stitches intersect. In the example below, I stretched the fabric on an embroidery hoop and used a water-soluble marking pen to draw a circle 1¹⁄₄ inches (3.2 cm) in diameter as a guide for the straight stitches, which are about ³⁄₁₆ inch (0.5 cm) apart.

1. Stitch a set of long, equally spaced, parallel straight stitches across the form. Turn the hoop 90 degrees, then repeat to stitch a set of straight stitches that run perpendicular to the first. The lattice grid is now complete.

2. Starting at a far corner of the grid, use a contrasting thread to stitch a small straight stitch over one of its intersecting points. Bring the thread up through the fabric on the other side of the same point of intersection to make a second straight stitch that overlaps the first. Bring the thread up at the closest intersecting point and repeat.

3. A completed lattice-couched circle.

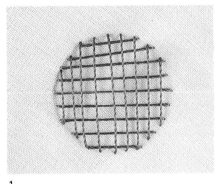

1

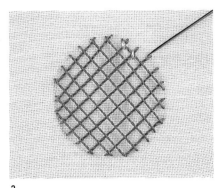

2

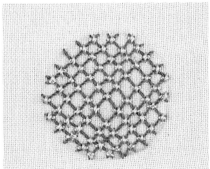

3

STEM STITCH

The stem stitch, which is usually used to outline rather than fill in a shape, consists of stitches that overlap at half-point intervals to make a continuous line. Both the length of the stitches in any given line and the side on which you work the stitches must be consistent. Always keep the ribbon or floss *beneath* the needle when making each stitch.

1. To start a line of stem stitches, come up at point A. Then, working in the opposite direction, go down at B and come up at C, keeping the ribbon or floss on one side of the outline.

2. Again changing direction, loop the ribbon or floss on the same side of the outline as in step 1, then go down at D and come up at E (the midpoint of the previous stitch).

3. As the needle is drawn through the fabric, the loop of the ribbon or floss will overlap the previous stitch. Continue working from top to bottom in the same direction until the outline is complete.

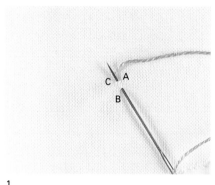

1

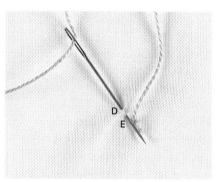

2

3

FRENCH KNOT AND PISTIL STITCH

With the French knot, the needle is twisted around the needle before both are pulled back through the fabric directly into the point where it was initially drawn. The pistil stitch is similar to the French knot, except that the wrapped needle is taken down a short distance away from the original point.

1. Bring the needle up through the fabric. Holding the ribbon taut, wind it behind the needle.

2. Take the ribbon over the needle, forming one complete wrap.

3. Keeping the wrapped ribbon close to the tip of the needle, place the needle into the fabric very close to point A (but not into it), then gently pull the ribbon through. Hold the knot in place until the stitch is completed.

4. A completed French knot.

5. To make a pistil stitch, wrap the ribbon or floss over the needle two or three times, holding it taut as you wind it. Determine the length of the stitch, then insert the needle back into the fabric. Slide the wrapped ribbon or floss down the needle to the fabric, then slowly pull the needle through.

6. A completed pistil stitch.

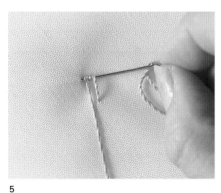

1

2

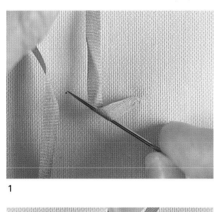

3

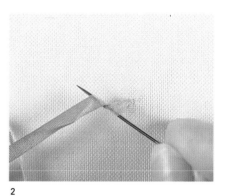

4

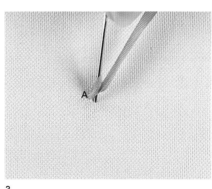

5

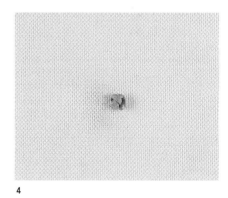

6

LAZY DAISY

The lazy daisy, which is also referred to as a detached chain stitch, is a standard embroidery stitch that lends itself well to silk ribbon embroidery. Note that the length of the lazy daisy's anchor stitch can be varied for a dramatic look.

By adding a straight stitch in a contrasting ribbon within the loop of the lazy daisy (see step 4), you can create a decorative lazy daisy. A decorative lazy daisy can even be worked in three colors—purple for the loop, white for the anchor stitch, and yellow for the straight stitch—to create stunning bearded irises.

1. Bring the needle and ribbon up through the fabric at point A. Keeping the ribbon loose and untwisted, make a loop. Go down at B (immediately adjacent to A) and back up at C so that the needle passes over the ribbon.

2. As the ribbon is pulled through, the loop will tighten.

3. Finish the loop with a small anchor stitch to complete the lazy daisy.

4. To make a decorative lazy daisy, add a straight stitch to the center of the completed lazy daisy using a second color of ribbon.

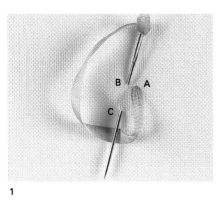

1

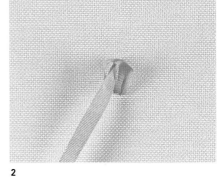

2

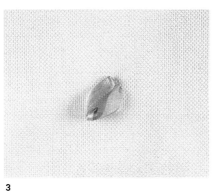

3

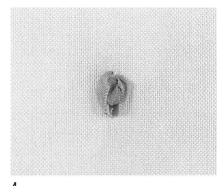

4

FEATHER STITCH

The feather stitch consists of a series of Y-shaped stitches (individually known as *fly stitches*) alternating from right to left. These stitches can be worked long or short to produce a variety of forms. The maidenhair stitch (see page 99) is just one variation.

1. Come up at point A. Working at an angle and curving the ribbon or floss beneath the needle, go down at B and come back up at C.

2. The resulting stitch makes the initial Y shape.

3. Working to the right of the first stitch, go down at D and come back up at E, curving the ribbon or floss beneath the needle.

4. The second Y is formed.

5. Working to the left of the preceding stitch, repeat step 3.

6. The third Y is formed. Add "branches" by continuing to alternate the stitches left and right.

7. A completed feather stitch. Finish the final Y with a small anchor stitch.

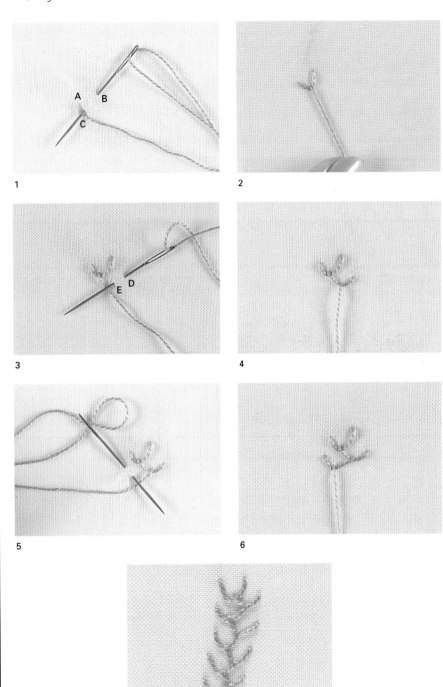

FRENCH KNOT LOOP STITCH

The French knot loop stitch begins as an incomplete straight stitch. Instead of pulling the ribbon flat against the surface of the fabric, it's left loose to form a little loop, which is then pierced with a French knot. The French knot can be stitched either at the center or at one end of the loop, with either ribbon or floss in the same or a contrasting color, or substituted with a bead or pearl. The French knot loop stitch is an easy way to create dimension, and works well as "filler" when stitching a large cluster of flowers.

1. Come up at point A and go down at B (about ⅛ inch [0.3 cm] from A).

2. Pull the ribbon through the fabric to form a loose loop.

3. Come up through the center of the loop with two strands of floss.

4. Double-wrap the needle with floss to make a French knot in the center of the loop.

5. A completed loop stitch.

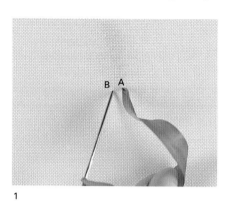

1

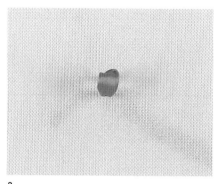

2

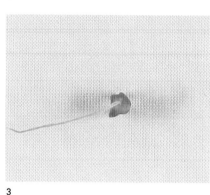

3

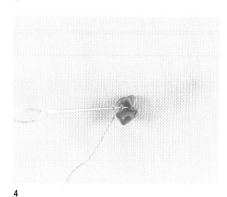

4

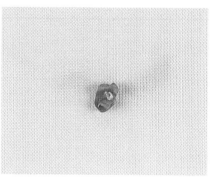

5

PLUME STITCH

The plume stitch is yet another variation on the loop. A series of connecting loops is made by piercing the front of one loop from the back of the fabric to form the next. As with the loop flower, you might need a laying tool to hold each loop in place as you work. A plume stitch can be finished with a straight stitch on the front or back of the fabric (see step 5), or on the front with a single-wrap French knot. This stitch is not a good choice for wearables.

1. Come up at point A and go down at B (about ⅛ inch [0.3 cm] from A).

2. Make a loop approximately ¼ inch (0.6 cm) in length.

3. Pierce the front of the preceding loop with the needle. If necessary, hold the loop in place with your thumb or a laying tool.

4. Draw the needle and ribbon through the loop, then go back down through the fabric. Repeat steps 3 and 4 to make additional loops.

5. A completed five-loop plume stitch, finished on the reverse with a straight stitch.

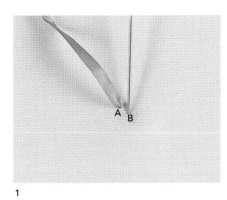

1

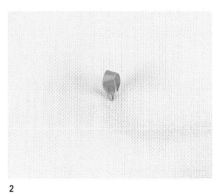

2

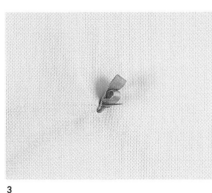

3

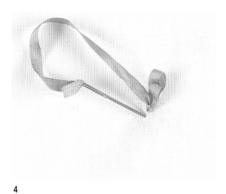

4

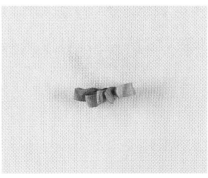

5

PUNCH NEEDLE

The lush, full loops made with a punch needle can add dimension and texture to your ribbon embroidery. The materials required for punch needle are few, portable, and very easy to use. Punch needles come in various sizes, and there is a gauge on the punch for adjusting the lengths of the loops. I have a large needle for 4mm ribbon, and three smaller ones that accommodate six strands, three strands, and one strand of embroidery floss, respectively. The ribbon or thread is pulled into the punch, through the center of the needle, and out again through the eye with a needle threader.

When working with a punch needle, you'll need a loosely woven fabric such as the 32-count aida cloth that I used for the demonstration. Because the grain of the fabric must be kept aligned, it should be mounted, drum-tight, on a plastic embroidery hoop. So that the loops appear on the front of the fabric, the punch needle is worked on the back. Simply draw an outline of the motif with a water-soluble marking pen and use it as a guide for stitching. Once you've used all the ribbon or thread in the needle, clip it off flush to the fabric on the back. The stitches will not come out.

Once you've established a comfortable rhythm, punch needlework is virtually effortless, providing a quick and easy way to enrich your designs.

A fantasy flower punched with 4mm silk ribbon and YLI Pearl Crown Rayon thread, a twisted fiber approximately equivalent in density to six strands of cotton embroidery floss. Embroidered embellishments include 4mm silk French knots and purple metallic braid loops stitched in the center of the flower, Mokuba 7mm pink cottonaire Japanese ribbon stitches stitched between each of the petals, with hand-dyed 4mm green silk lazy daisy leaves and purple metallic braid pistil stitches.

1. Threading the Punch Needle. Insert the threader through the point of the needle and slide it all the way to the other end of the plastic holder. Place the ribbon into the threader and pull it through.

2. Insert the threader into the eye on the side of the needle and pull the ribbon through it.

3. The threaded punch needle.

4. Using the Punch Needle. To make a simple flower, draw four petals on the back of loosely woven fabric mounted on a hoop. Holding the needle at a slight angle, insert it into the fabric and push down until it stops. Pull the needle back toward you without lifting it off of the fabric. Repeat.

5. Continue punching within the outline while aligning stitches side-by-side.

6. The loops will appear on the right side of the fabric.

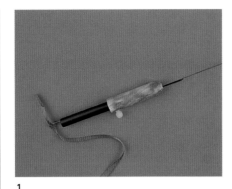

1

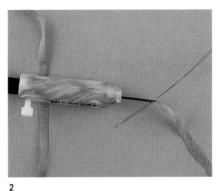

2

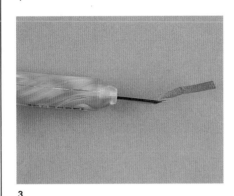

3

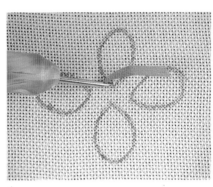

4

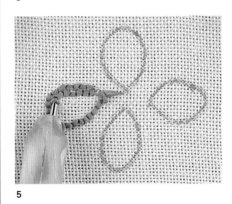

5

6

STITCHING FAUNA

(Opposite) An intricate peacock stitched with decorative lazy daisies, straight stitches, couching, satin stitches, and French knots in an array of ribbons, threads, and flosses. (Right) In this detail from the front cover, a fish's body is stenciled with Lumiere fabric paint (see page 109) and outlined with stem stitches.

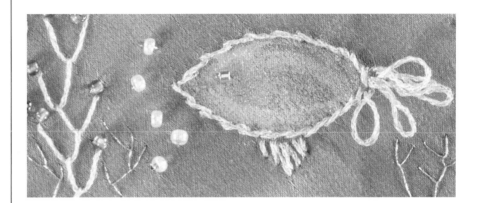

In this chapter, the basic embroidery stitches demonstrated in the preceding chapter are used to create beautiful insects, birds, marine animals, and fantasy animals, all of which are well within the reach of the beginning stitcher. In some instances, stitches were further embellished with punch needle, gathered ribbon, and appliqué. These motifs require an investment of time and effort, but the sumptuous mixture of color and texture are well worth it. Create your own animals by investigating different sources; for example, adapt jewelry from a gift catalog or use basic animal shapes from a children's coloring book.

The materials and colors listed for each motif were used to create the example shown in the accompanying photograph, and should be viewed as suggestions rather than requirements. A word of advice on vintage materials: Although they may look fine when purchased in skeins, due to their age they may simply disintegrate once stitching has begun. Test all your vintage materials to make sure they can handle the stress of stitching before incorporating them into a motif.

DRAGONFLY

STITCHES

Straight stitch

Stem stitch

MATERIALS

Fabric

6-inch (15.2-cm) square
of silver silk

**Metallic Ribbon,
1/8 inch (0.32 cm)
wide**

1 spool royal blue

1 spool aqua

1 spool white

Thread and Braid

1 spool #4 white very
fine metallic braid

Nymo beading thread

Embellishments

Two 8mm red metallic
beads

1. Using the method described on page 46, transfer the pattern to the fabric.
2. Use royal blue, aqua, and white metallic ribbon to stitch straight stitches within the wings.
3. Outline the wings with stem stitches stitched with the white braid.
4. Create a webbed pattern within the wings by stitching straight stitches with the white braid.
5. Use royal blue metallic ribbon to stem stitch the dragonfly's body between the wings.
6. For the eyes, use the Nymo thread to stitch a red metallic bead on either side of the royal blue stem stitching.

The completed dragonfly.

WASP

Stem stitch
Japanese ribbon stitch
Satin stitch
Straight stitch

MATERIALS

Fabric

6-inch (15.2-cm) square
of gold silk

Silk Ribbon

1 yard (0.9 m) 4mm
blue

Thread and Braid

1 spool #8 fine gold
metallic braid

1 spool Kelly green
rayon thread

Nymo beading thread

Embellishments

1 package Mill Hill
silver glass beads

2 red glass beads

1. Using the method described on page 46, transfer the pattern to the fabric.
2. Use the gold braid to outline the wings, head, and thorax with stem stitching.
3. Fill the top corner of each of the four wings with Japanese ribbon stitches in blue ribbon.
4. Stitch part of the wings and the thorax with satin stitches using green thread.
5. Satin stitch the accents in the wings and the head with the gold braid.
6. Use the Nymo thread to fill the remaining wing segments with silver beads.
7. Straight stitch the abdomen with blue silk ribbon.
8. Use gold braid to indicate sections within the abdomen by stitching two immediately adjacent straight stitches at regular intervals along its length.
9. Stem stitch three legs underneath the thorax using gold braid.
10. To make the eyes, use the Nymo thread to stitch a red glass on the top and side of the head.

The completed wasp.

BEE

STITCHES

Couching

Satin stitch

Straight stitch

MATERIALS

Fabric

6-inch (15.2-cm) square of red-and-gold silk shot

Metallic Ribbon, 1/8 inch (0.32 cm) wide

1 spool gold

1 spool black

1 spool silver

Thread

1 skein gold rayon thread, 1/8 inch (0.32 cm) wide

Nymo beading thread

Embellishments

26 red metallic glass beads

1. Using the method described on page 46, transfer the pattern to the fabric.
2. Outline the wings and body by couching gold ribbon with Nymo thread.
3. Using alternating rows of black ribbon and gold thread, fill in the abdomen with satin stitches.
4. Orienting the stitches vertically, satin stitch both wings with silver ribbon.
5. Create the webbed pattern within the wings by stitching long straight stitches of gold ribbon over the silver satin stitches.
6. For the head, stitch two straight stitches in black within the couched gold ribbon outline, and two in silver ribbon immediately above it.
7. Stitch the legs and antennae with one straight stitch of gold ribbon each.
8. Fill in the thorax with red metallic glass beads stitched with Nymo thread.

The completed bee.

BUTTERFLY

STITCHES

Couching
Japanese ribbon stitch
Straight stitch
Fly stitch

MATERIALS

Fabric

6-inch (15.2-cm) square of ivory silk broadcloth

Ribbon

1 yard (0.9 m) 4mm hand-dyed silk, variegated in shades of purple and bronze

1 card gold rayon, 1/8 inch (0.32 cm) wide

1 spool purple metallic, 1/8 inch (0.32 cm) wide

Braid

1 spool #8 fine purple
1 spool #8 fine gold

Thread

Nymo beading thread

Embellishments

1 tube burgundy Delica beads

1. Using the method described on page 46, transfer the pattern to the fabric.
2. Outline the exterior and interior contours of the butterfly's wings and stitch the antennae by couching the purple braid with Nymo thread.
3. Use the variegated silk ribbon to stitch parallel Japanese ribbon stitches within the interior contour of the wings, then to stitch the abdomen with small straight stitches.
4. Add a small straight stitch of gold ribbon between each Japanese ribbon stitch.
5. Stitch two straight stitches of gold ribbon at the edge of each lower wing lobe.
6. Using the purple metallic ribbon, add a straight stitch between every other pair of Japanese ribbon stitches within the interior contour of the wings.
7. Using gold braid, create webbing within the interior contour of the wings by stitching fly stitches, then add straight stitches at regular intervals along the length of the ribbon abdomen and within the lower wing lobes.
8. Use purple braid to add fly stitch webbing within the lower wing lobes.
9. With red Delica beads stitched with Nymo thread, densely fill the head and the extension of the abdomen, then randomly stitch any spaces within the exterior contour of the wings. Stitch a single bead at the end of each antenna.

The completed butterfly.

BABY CHICK

STITCHES

Punch needle
Straight stitch
Stem stitch
Satin stitch

MATERIALS

Fabric

6-inch (15.2-cm) square
of 32-count pale green
aida cloth

Ribbon

12 inches (30.5 cm)
2mm variegated lemon
yellow silk

Thread, Floss, and
Braid

1 skein lemon yellow
cotton floss

1 spool #8 fine gold
braid

Nymo beading thread

Embellishments

1 green Delica bead

Miscellaneous

Plastic hoop, 4 inches
(10.2 cm) in diameter

Punch needle (needle
should accommodate
6 strands of floss or
2mm silk ribbon)

1. Using the method described on page 46, transfer the pattern to the front of the mounted fabric, then draw the body on the back. The fabric should be stretched very tightly and its grain precisely aligned.
2. Punch-needle the entire body with three strands of yellow floss.
3. For the tail, stitch three or four long straight stitches with yellow ribbon.
4. Stem stitch the legs and feet with the gold braid.
5. Use the gold braid to add a few straight stitches within the ribbon tail.
6. Satin stitch the beak with gold braid.
7. For the eye, stitch the bead into place with Nymo thread.

The completed baby chick.

TOUCAN

STITCHES

Stem stitch
Japanese ribbon stitch
Straight stitch
Satin stitch

MATERIALS

Fabrics

6-inch (15.2-cm) square of ivory broadcloth

Two small scraps of Ultrasuede in yellow and royal blue

Silk Ribbon

18 inches (45.7 cm)

4mm Kelly green

4mm burgundy

10 inches (25.4 cm)

4mm blue

4mm yellow

Thread and Braid

1 skein Kelly green rayon thread

1 spool of #8 fine gold braid

18 inches (45.7 cm) black metallic braid

Nymo beading thread

Embellishments

1 package of Mill Hill silver glass beads

1 8mm burgundy triangle glass bead

1. Using the method described on page 46, transfer the pattern to the broadcloth.
2. Following the instructions on page 100, appliqué the Ultrasuede remnants to the broadcloth with tiny stitches of Nymo thread.
3. Outline the beak, body, and the area around the eye and chest by stem stitching with gold braid.
4. Use the green, yellow, and burgundy ribbons to stitch Japanese ribbon stitch wing feathers.
5. Straight stitch burgundy ribbon over the beak where it meets the head, then stitch one Japanese ribbon stitch near the tip of the beak.
6. Satin stitch the eye area with Kelly green thread.
7. Using gold braid, stitch the claws with short straight stitches.
8. Use the black braid to stitch the perch with horizontal straight stitches.
9. Stitch Japanese ribbon stitch tail feathers with green, blue, and burgundy ribbon.
10. Add long, loose straight stitches of gold braid among the feathers.
11. Stitch the burgundy triangle bead in the center of the green eye area.
12. Fill in the chest area by stitching the silver glass beads with Nymo thread.

The completed toucan.

CRAB

STITCHES

Satin stitch
Stem stitch

MATERIALS

Fabric

6-inch (15.2-cm) square
of painted and alcohol-
treated cotton muslin

Ribbon

1 yard (0.9 m) 4mm
hand-dyed orange
variegated silk

Thread and Braid

1 skein orange metallic
braid

1 spool #8 fine red-
orange braid

Nymo beading thread

Embellishments

2 gold beads

1. Using the method described on page 46, transfer the pattern to the fabric.
2. Satin stitch the body with orange ribbon.
3. Stem stitch the outline of the body with orange metallic braid.
4. Satin stitch the claws and antennae with red-orange braid.
5. Use the Nymo to stitch a gold bead at the end of each antenna.

The completed crab.

SEAHORSE

STITCHES

Stem stitch

Satin stitch

Japanese ribbon stitch

MATERIALS

Fabric

6-inch (15.2-cm) square of silk broadcloth muslin

Silk Ribbon

2 yards (1.8 m) 4mm hand-dyed variegated rose

1¼ inches (3.2 cm) 13mm hand-dyed variegated rose bias-cut

Thread

1 skein rose marlitt rayon thread

Nymo beading thread

Embellishments

1 package frosted rose Mill Hill glass beads

3 rose bugle beads

1 green Delica glass bead

1. Using the method described on page 46, transfer the pattern to the fabric.
2. Stem stitch the outline of the body with one strand of rose marlitt.
3. Use the 4mm silk ribbon to fill the body with satin stitches.
4. Satin stitch the head with one strand of rose marlitt.
5. To make the eye, stitch the green bead with Nymo thread.
6. Use Nymo thread to stitch a row of frosted rose glass beads down the seahorse's spine.
7. Stitch a row of horizontal Japanese ribbon stitches along the spine of seahorse with 4mm silk ribbon.
8. Following the instructions on page 82, use the Nymo thread to gather the bias-cut ribbon to a length of ¾ inch (1.9 cm). Turn under the gathered edge and tack it to the seahorse's lower back.
9. Stitch the three bugle beads over bias-cut silk fin.

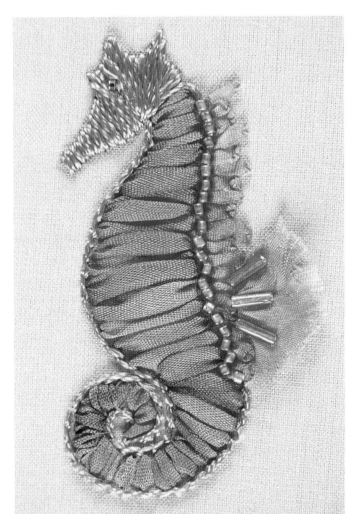

The completed seahorse.

FISH

STITCHES

Couching
Straight stitch
Lattice couching

MATERIALS

Fabrics

8-inch (20.3-cm) square
of peach moiré fabric
5-inch (12.7-cm) square
of iridescent ivory fabric

Ribbon

4 inches (10.2 cm)
green ombré,
1½ inches (3.8 cm)
wide
1 yard (0.9 cm) salmon
organdy
18 inches (45.7 cm)
4mm salmon-and-green
chevron ombré

Thread

18 inches (45.7 cm)
salmon chenille thread
1 skein dark metal
thread
1 skein salmon marlitt
Nymo beading thread

Embellishments

1 small polished black
rock bead

1. Using the method described on page 46, transfer the pattern to the moiré fabric.
2. Following the instructions on page 100, fold the iridescent fabric in half wrong sides together and appliqué it to the moiré fabric to create the fish's body.
3. Gather the green ombré ribbon with Nymo thread (see page 82). Turn under the gathered end and stitch it to end of the body to make the tail fin.
4. Outline the entire body by couching the salmon chenille thread with the metal thread.
5. Use salmon organdy ribbon to straight stitch the pelvic and anal fins.
6. Straight stitch the dorsal fins with the salmon-and-green chevron ribbon.
7. Add long straight stitches of metal thread between the straight stitches of the anal and dorsal fins.
8. To create the scales, lattice-couch straight stitches of one strand of salmon rayon thread with the metal thread.
9. Use Nymo thread to stitch the bead in place for the eye.

The completed fish.

SEASHELL

STITCHES

Japanese ribbon stitch
Straight stitch
Satin stitch
Stem stitch
Lazy daisy

MATERIALS

Fabric

8-inch (20.3-cm) square of pink 32-count aida cloth

Ribbon

2 yards (1.8 m)

7mm burgundy raysheen

7mm burgundy organdy

French picot-edge hot pink ombré silk

4mm hot pink variegated silk

1 yard (0.9 m)

4mm pink ribbon

Thread and Yarn

1 spool hot pink variegated yarn

1 skein lilac marlitt

1 skein hot pink marlitt

Embellishments

1 package Delica burgundy frosted beads

1. Using the method described on page 46, transfer the pattern to the fabric.
2. Use the burgundy raysheen ribbon to stitch vertical Japanese ribbon stitches in the uppermost band of the shell.
3. Use the burgundy organdy ribbon to stitch vertical Japanese ribbon stitches in the second band of the shell.
4. Stitch a vertical row of straight stitches in the third band using the picot-edge ribbon.
5. Stitch the next two bands of the shell with vertical straight stitches using 4mm variegated hot pink ribbon.
6. Use the variegated yarn to fill most of the shell's base with vertical satin stitches.
7. Use the lilac marlitt to satin stitch a highlight on the right side of the shell base.
8. Stitch a row of satin stitches along the contour of the shell's base with hot pink marlitt.
9. Stem stitch the stems with the variegated yarn.
10. Stitch a hot pink lazy daisy at tip of each stem.
11. Use the Nymo thread to tack the 4mm pink ribbon and the beads into place. As you twist and curl the ribbon, tack it in place with a bead. Use 18 beads on each side of the shell.
12. Stitch a row of beads between the lowest band of ribbon and the yarn.

The completed seashell.

SEAGOAT

STITCHES

Stem stitch

French knot

Twisted Japanese
ribbon stitch

Japanese ribbon stitch

Satin stitch

Straight stitch

MATERIALS

Fabrics

8-inch (20.3-cm) square
of white linen

3-inch (7.6-cm) square
of handpainted bias-cut
silk in teal green and
hot pink

Silk Ribbon

1 yard (0.9 m) 4mm
hand-dyed hot pink and
purple variegated

Thread and Braid

1 skein hot pink marlitt

1 spool #8 fine silver
braid

Nymo beading thread

Embellishments

34 glass beads in hot
pink, gold, and teal

2 teal bugle beads

1 10mm hot pink glass
bead

1. Using the method described on page 46, transfer the pattern to the fabric.
2. Cut out the body of the seagoat (excluding its head, legs, and tail) from the bias-cut silk. Following the instructions on page 100, appliqué the bias-cut silk to the linen to create the body.
3. Outline the entire pattern with stem stitches in one strand of marlitt.
4. Use one strand of marlitt to fill in the legs and tail with French knots.
5. To make the mane, cut the bias-cut silk into six pieces each 1¹/₂ inches (3.8 cm) long and ¹/₄ inch (0.6 cm) wide, fray their edges, and tack them down with tiny stitches of Nymo thread along the back of the seagoat's head. Give some of the ribbons a single twist.
6. Using 4mm variegated hot pink ribbon, add three or four very loose one-twist twisted Japanese ribbon stitches within the mane.
7. Add a line of French knots in ribbon where the legs meet the body.
8. Stitch Japanese ribbon stitches in ribbon where the tail meets the body.
9. Satin stitch the head and horn with one strand of marlitt.
10. Satin stitch the hooves and tail with silver braid, then use the braid to add a few widely spaced straight stitches over the satin stitches of the horn.
11. Use the Nymo thread to randomly stitch hot pink glass beads among the French knots in the legs and tail.
12. Stitch glass beads between the straight stitches on the horn.
13. Randomly stitch glass beads and the two bugle beads within the mane.
14. For the eye, stitch the large pink glass and two small beads.

The completed seagoat.

DRAGON

STITCHES
Couching
French knot
Japanese ribbon stitch
Straight stitch
Twisted Japanese
ribbon stitch

MATERIALS
Fabric
8- × 10-inch
(20.3- × 25.4-cm)
piece of red-and-gold
shot silk
Ribbon
2 yards (1.8 m)
4mm gold silk
7mm gold Heirloom
Sylk
1 yard (0.9 m)
4mm avocado green
Heirloom Sylk
4mm red Heirloom
Sylk
Thread, Floss, and Braid
1 spool medium gold
braid
1 skein gold rayon floss
Nymo beading thread
Embellishments
39 8mm gold beads

1. Using the method described on page 46, transfer the pattern to the fabric.
2. Outline the entire body by couching the gold braid with Nymo thread.
3. Stitch French knots throughout the body with 4mm gold ribbon and two strands of gold floss. Stitch French knots in 7mm gold ribbon along the belly between the legs and where the chest meets the front leg.
4. Use the Nymo thread to stitch beads along the back of the neck and in the chest, belly, back leg, and tail.
5. Stitch Japanese ribbon stitches along the back of the head, back, and tail, within the chest, and on the backs of the legs using 4mm gold ribbon.
6. Use two strands of gold floss to straight stitch the snout.
7. Add straight stitches in gold braid in the claws and lower jaw.
8. For the mane, stitch twisted Japanese ribbon stitches using green and red ribbons, then add three long, loose twisted straight stitches of gold braid.
9. Add Japanese ribbon stitch "fringes" in green ribbon to the lower jaw, the back of the front leg, and on the last curve of the tail.
10. Adorn the end of the tail with Japanese ribbon stitches with 4mm gold and red ribbons.

The completed dragon.

STITCHING FLORA

(Opposite) This small bouquet of gathered forms (see pages 82–86) includes one purple and two two-tone bias-cut ruffled flowers, two 9mm green ribbon leaves, and a 4mm pink silk filler ruffle. Three 6mm pearls were added as finishing touches. (Right) An assortment of ruched and gathered flowers.

As even those with just a limited knowledge of ribbon embroidery can affirm, basic embroidery stitches can be combined to create beautiful flowers as well as animals. Also shown in this chapter are easy techniques for folding, gathering, and ruching ribbon, as well as creating bias tubing to make dimensional forms.

You can find inspiration for flowers in many places. I base many of my floral designs on the photographs I take of the flowers in my garden.

BASIC FLOWER STITCHES

TWO-RIBBON SPIRAL ROSE

I developed the two-ribbon spiral rose especially for this book. To begin, thread a needle with two 12-inch (30.5-cm) lengths of 4mm silk ribbon, then knot each end.

1. Bring the ribbons up through to the front of the fabric at point A, then begin twisting them. Stop twisting once the ribbons have folded in half against the fabric.

2. Take the needle back down through the fabric immediately adjacent to A. Pull the ribbons through slowly until there are about 2 inches (5 cm) on the back of the fabric.

3. Tie off and cut the ribbons on the back of the fabric. A small "bud" is formed at the point where the needle was drawn through.

4. To complete the rose, wrap the twisted ribbons around the bud and secure them with several tiny stitches of Nymo beading thread. Hide the folded end of the ribbons under the rose and tack it down with a small stitch.

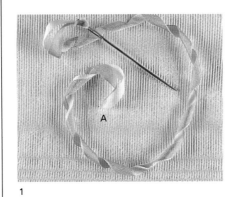

1

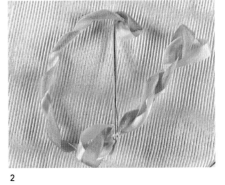

2

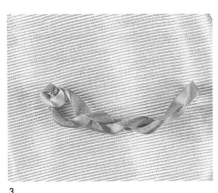

3

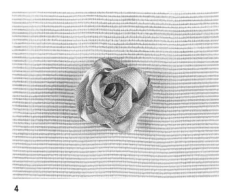

4

1. Using two strands of floss to match the ribbon, bring the needle through the fabric at point A. Go down at B and come up at C, bringing the tip of the needle over the thread to form a Y shape. Finish the Y by bringing the needle down through the fabric below C so that the stem of the Y is the same length as its diagonals.

2. To create the five spokes that will serve as the foundation for the rose, make two straight stitches on either side of the Y the same length as the Y's stem and diagonals. Securely knot off the floss on the back.

3. Bring the ribbon through the fabric between two spokes and as close to the center as possible.

4. Working in a counterclockwise direction, begin to weave the ribbon under and over the spokes.

5. When the spokes have been wound once, adjust the ribbon to conceal the axis.

6. Continue to weave the ribbon, working loosely and allowing the ribbon to twist and turn.

7. When the spokes are completely hidden, take the needle down through the fabric and secure the ribbon with a knot.

SPIDER WEB ROSE

A favorite among beginners because it is so easy to execute, the spider web rose is formed by winding the ribbon around an odd number of spokes until they're no longer visible. The underlying framework of the sample stitch shown below is a single feather stitch (more commonly known as a *fly stitch*) that is bolstered with two straight stitches to form a five-spoke wheel.

To enhance the look of your spider web rose, make the first two revolutions with a light shade and the last two with a darker one. As delightful finishing touches on a completed rose, stitch two or three French knots or add a single seed pearl in its center.

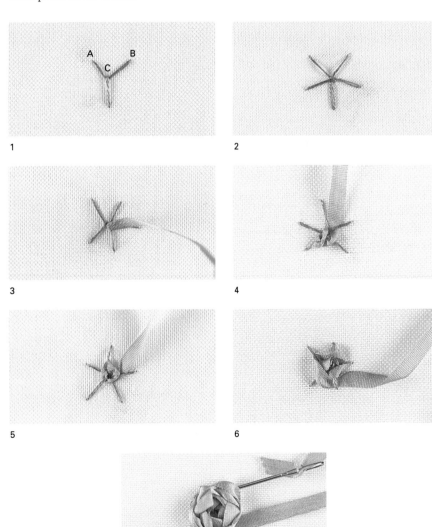

1

2

3

4

5

6

7

LOOP AND RUFFLE STITCH FLOWERS

This frilly stitch, which works best with 4mm ribbons, is perfect for embellishing small-scale projects such as doll's dresses and miniatures.

1. Thread a short length of 4mm ribbon, then make four or five short running stitches in the end of the ribbon.

2. Insert the needle into the fabric and pull it through.

3. The completed loop stitch flower (left). For a fuller, ruffled flower, increase the number of running stitches and space them more widely.

4. Several completed loop and ruffle stitch flowers stitched with 4mm Heirloom Sylk variegated ribbons.

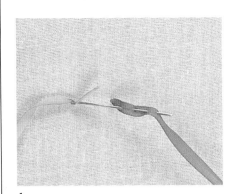

1

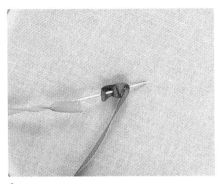

2

3

4

FOLDED RIBBON

Accessible even to the avowed nonstitcher, folding takes ribbon embroidery a step beyond stitching toward slightly more complex ribbon manipulation techniques such as gathering (see page 82), ruching (page 87), and tubes (page 88). In this section, the folding technique is used to make roses, leaves, buds, and petals.

FOLDED LEAVES AND BUDS

When folding leaves and buds, always start with at least 3 inches (7.6 cm) of ribbon. Before attaching leaves and buds to fabric, trim off excess ribbon; if the ribbon has a tendency to fray or if the leaf or bud will be used on a garment, treat the ends with Fray Check (see page 46).

1. Mentally divide the length of ribbon in half, then fold one half over the other. Using Nymo thread or floss in a matching color, stitch small stitches across the entire width of the fold and through both sides of the ribbon, making sure you catch the selvage.

2. To complete the leaf, pull the thread to gather the ribbon, then knot it off. In this example, double-sided silk-satin ribbon hand-dyed in celadon green was used.

3. To create a bud and leaf, fold a piece of ribbon as directed in step 1, then fold a piece of green ribbon over it. Working from one side to the other, stitch across the width of the ribbon, catching all the layers and the selvage. Gather the ribbon, then knot off the thread securely.

1

2

3

1. Tightly roll the ribbon three times.

2. Holding the ribbon roll firmly, secure its layers by making several small stitches at one end with knotted floss. Leaving the floss attached, proceed to the next step.

3. Holding the roll between thumb and forefinger, fold the top edge of the ribbon back and down.

4. Wrap the folded ribbon once around the center roll to form the first petal.

5. Secure the first petal by stitching through all the layers at the bottom of the roll.

6. Repeat steps 3 through 5 to make two or three more wraps. Secure each wrap at the bottom of the rose with two tight stitches. After completing the final wrap, trim the ribbon to leave a 1/2-inch (1.3-cm) tail. Bring the needle up through the base of the rose to the center, then back down to the base. Repeat. Finish the base with two stitches, then knot off and cut the floss. Trim the ribbon again, this time to leave an 1/8-inch (0.3-cm) piece. Attach the rose to fabric with several small stitches.

7. This folded ribbon rose and bud were made with hand-dyed double-sided 1-inch (2.5-cm) silk-satin ribbon.

FOLDED ROSE

Due to the ribbon's slippery texture this folded form can be tricky at first, but with practice it can be made quite quickly. The smallest widths of ribbon that can be used to make this rose are 7mm silk ribbon and 5/8-inch (1.6-cm) double-sided satin ribbon. For an average-size rose, you'll need about 7 to 9 inches (17.8 to 22.9 cm) of ribbon. When working with 1- or 1 5/8-inch (2.5- or 4.1-cm) ribbon you'll need a longer length, depending on the size of the rose you want to make.

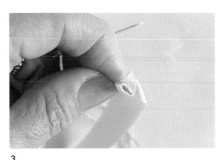

1

2

3

4

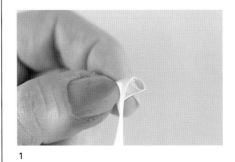

5

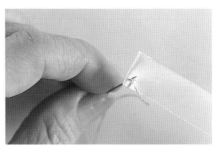

6

7

FOLDED MULTIPETAL FLOWER

By using the basic folded leaf technique with brightly colored ribbon and repeating the leaf form several times, you can make a dazzling dahlia or chrysanthemum, or experiment by creating a "fantasy flower."

1. Use the instructions in step 1 of "Folded Leaves and Buds" (page 79) to fold and gather each petal. Trim the leftover ribbon close to the stitching. Repeat to make as many petals as needed to create your flower.

2. This fantasy flower consists of sixteen folded petals in 1-inch (2.5-cm) hand-dyed organdy ribbon stitched around a coiled center of hot pink nylon bias tubing (see page 89). Begin by stitching the bias tube to the fabric with Nymo beading thread, then stitch the uppermost ring of petals around it. Add succeeding rings of petals by tucking them behind one another, then stitching them into place. Finish the flower by stitching a circle of beads around the circumference and in the center of the tubing.

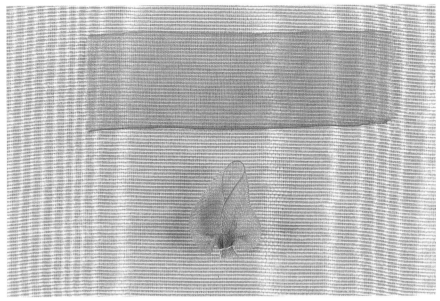

1

2

GATHERED RIBBON

The gathering technique consists of stitching a straight line of evenly spaced running stitches lengthwise along a piece of ribbon, then "gathering" it into a shape by pulling the thread tightly or by scrunching the ribbon down on the thread. Depending on where the stitches are made along the ribbon's width—either straight down its center, along either selvage, or along a folded edge—and how tightly the ribbon is scrunched, a variety of forms can be created, including ruffles, flowers, and leaves.

The applications for small pieces of gathered bias-cut ribbon are limitless, and offer a striking visual contrast to carefully made embroidery stitches. In this book, bias-cut gathered ribbon has been used to create a seahorse's fin (see page 69), an iris's beard (see page 92), and some fish fins (see the front cover). Note, however, that bias-cut ribbons less than 1/2 inch (1.3 cm) wide have a tendency to break after their edges have been frayed.

Regardless of where on the ribbon's width the running stitches are placed, always begin by bringing the needle up through the ribbon at one end and taking a straight stitch and then a backstitch before making the first running stitch. This step stabilizes the ribbon and prevents the thread from pulling out when it is gathered.

When your gathered form is complete, incorporate it into your stitch design with a neutral color of Nymo beading thread.

1. To gather a small filler ruffle, stitch running stitches down the center of 6 inches (15.2 cm) of 4mm silk ribbon with Nymo beading thread.

2. The gathered ruffle. The length of the ruffle will vary, depending on how tightly it's scrunched. Once you've determined the ruffle's length, knot off the thread, then stitch it to the fabric.

3. The same method applies to bias-cut ribbon. This piece of 1/2-inch (1.3-cm) bias-cut ribbon, which was cut from a 2-inch (5-cm) strip of crepe silk, was handpainted with Pēbēo Setasilk silk paints.

4. Once bias-cut ribbon has been gathered, you can fray its edges by pricking them with a needle.

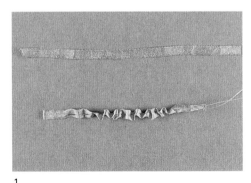

1

2

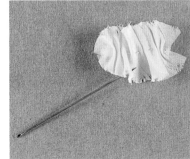
3

4

SIMPLE GATHERED FLOWER

To make a simple flower, finish the ends of 4 to 5 inches (10 to 12.7 cm) of ribbon by stitching about ⅛ inch (0.3 cm) to the back with Nymo beading thread or two strands of matching floss, then take a line of running stitches along one selvage. Shape the ribbon into a circle so that the two ends meet, right sides facing, then whip stitch them together, starting at one end and knotting off at the other.

1. Stitch running stitches along one selvage.

2. Gather the ribbon, then knot off the thread.

3. Coil the ribbon into a circle and whip stitch the ends together.

4. The completed gathered flower, made with ⅝-inch (1.6-cm) handpainted Petersham, with a three-bead center and lazy daisy leaves stitched with two colors of variegated Heirloom Sylk.

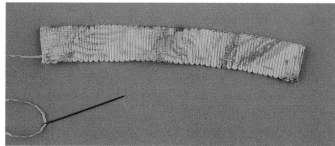

1

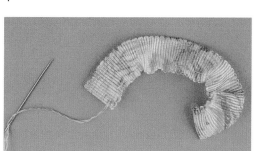

2

3

4

RUFFLED GATHERED FLOWER

To make a ruffled flower, fold 4 to 5 inches (10 to 12.7 cm) of at least ¹/₂-inch (1.3-cm) ribbon in half selvage to selvage, right sides together, then take running stitches through both sides of the fold. Gather the ribbon, knot off the thread, wind the ribbon into a circle, and stitch it to the fabric. To make a larger, fuller flower, use a longer and/or wider ribbon.

1. Fold the ribbon in half so that the selvages meet, then stitch running stitches along the fold.

2. A completed ruffled flower, made with 8 inches (20.3 cm) of 1¹/₄-inch (3.2-cm) two-tone bias-cut ribbon. The edges were frayed to produce a fringed effect.

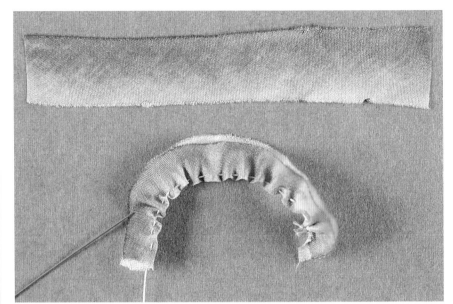

1

2

GATHERED LEAVES

The procedure for making leaves is yet another variation on the basic gathering technique. Take 2¹/₂ inches (6.4 cm) of ¹/₂-inch (1.3-cm) bias-cut green ribbon and fold it in half, right sides together. Take a line of running stitches along one selvage through both sides of the ribbon. Gather the ribbon, then knot off the thread. To create the leaf, gently pull open the unstitched side of the ribbon to reveal the leaf.

1. Fold the ribbon in half, right sides together, then stitch a line of running stitches along one selvage through both sides.

2. Gather the ribbon, knot off the thread, then open the unstitched side of the ribbon.

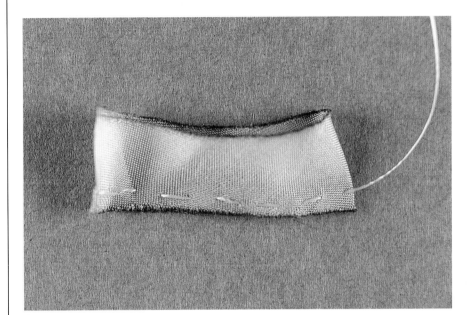

1

2

GATHERING OTHER MATERIALS

Once you've mastered a few ribbon-gathering techniques, you'll want to try your new-found skill with other materials. Experiment with wire-edge ribbon, or recycle some of the trims you either have hidden away in your sewing box or can find at any fabric and notions store and many craft stores. Note that such trims can even be used with some of the basic ribbon embroidery stitches shown on pages 48–57. Use a #16 needle with these wider, bulkier trims.

This fantasy flower was made from a 14-inch (35.6-cm) length of handpainted 1-inch (2.5-cm) wire-edge white polyester ribbon with metallic edging. The ribbon was gathered, shaped into a circle leaving a 1/2-inch (1.3-cm) opening, and tacked to the fabric by pinching 1 inch of the ribbon, pulling it into the center of the opening, and stitching it into place. Five 1/2-inch (1.3-cm) purple bugle beads and five glass beads were stitched around the circumference of the opening, then mauve and pink organdy ribbons were brought up through its center. Stitched among the gathers are Japanese ribbon stitches and small beads.

An collection of gathered and stitched flowers made using a variety of trims. (Clockwise from top left) A gathered flower made with Flexi-lace seam binding; gathered flowers in yellow rickrack and purple ribbon and a coiled flower made with medium rickrack and double-fold bias tape; and a stitch flower featuring loop flowers in purple seam binding tape over purple organdy Japanese ribbon stitches.

RUCHED RIBBON

A variation on gathering, ruching was first developed during the Victorian era and is experiencing something of a resurgence in popularity. This technique, which was originally used with strips of fabric, makes attractive flowers and borders and is an excellent complement to traditional ribbon embroidery.

Instead of being stitched in a straight line, the running stitches are stitched in a repetitive zigzag or scalloped configuration. To simplify this process, which may intimidate beginners, and maximize the accuracy of your stitching, I recommend using a plastic ruching template, such as the Mini Ruching Edge; if you prefer, you can cut your own template from a piece of stiff cardboard. Simply lay the template over the ribbon, then use a fade-away fabric marking pen to trace the guidelines on the ribbon. Use floss or Nymo beading thread to stitch over the marks with small straight running stitches. Once you've become comfortable with the technique, you can try stitching directly on the fabric without guidelines.

1. A ruching edge has been used to draw a scalloped guideline on a 13mm handpainted silk ribbon.

2. The same ribbon after stitching and gathering.

3. This coiled flower features zigzag-ruched silk-satin ribbon handpainted with Delta Starlite Dye Shimmering Fabric Color paints.

4. This pansy was made by scallop-ruching a 1/2-inch-wide (1.3 cm) strip of handpainted velvet. The petals were stitched into shape, then the flower was tacked to the fabric with Nymo thread. Two strands of rayon floss in purple and yellow were used to add straight stitches to three of the petals, and three 8mm gold beads were stitched in the center. The leaves were made with Japanese ribbon stitches in 9mm hand-dyed organdy.

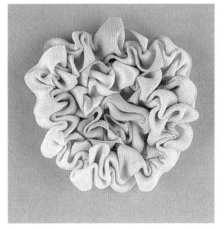

1

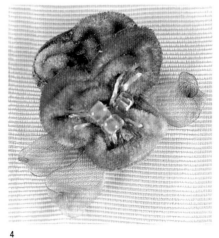

2

3

4

TUBES

Quite simply, a tube is a piece of ribbon or fabric that has been stitched into a cylindrical shape. Tubes are easy to make and can be used for a variety of decorative purposes.

How you plan to use the tube will dictate whether you use standard ribbon or bias-cut ribbon or fabric to make one. If you're making a small form that requires just a short tube—one that's no longer than 2 inches (5 cm)—you can use standard ribbon. If you're making a flower or other motif for which a long tube is needed, you must use bias-cut ribbon or fabric. If you tried to make a long tube with standard ribbon, you wouldn't be able to work with it; the ribbon's warp and weft would ripple and buckle, preventing it from draping properly.

In addition to the examples shown below and on the opposite page, tubes can also be seen in the center of a daffodil (see page 91) and on the front of an appliquéd blouse (page 128).

PODS

To make a tube for a pod or other small form, use 1¹/₂ to 2 inches (3.8 to 5 cm) of ribbon at least 13mm wide. Stitch the cut ends of the ribbon, right sides together, using about an ¹/₈-inch (0.32-cm) seam allowance. Flatten both edges of the seam toward one side with your finger, then turn the tube inside out.

1. To create a pod, first make a short tube. Gather the ribbon along one selvage and, starting at the seam, begin stitching the end of the tube closed. Stuff the tube generously with wool batting or polyester fiberfill.

2. To complete the pod, stitch the other end of the tube closed about ¹/₄ inch (0.6 cm) from the top, then knot off the thread securely. This example features 1¹/₂-inch (3.8-cm) silk ribbon painted with Pēbēo Setasilk silk paints.

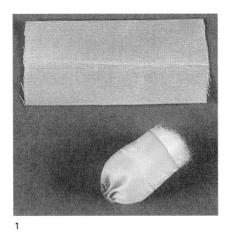

1

2

1. Fold a piece of bias-cut silk ribbon or fabric in half lengthwise and stitch it into a long tube using an $1/8$-inch (0.32-cm) seam allowance. Slip the stitched tube over the Fasturn cylinder, leaving $1/2$ inch (1.3 cm) of the tube extended over the end.

2. Insert the wire through the cylinder.

3. Hold the tube on the metal cylinder as you pierce the overhanging piece with the hooked end of the wire. As you slowly draw the wire back out of the cylinder, push the remaining tube down toward the end.

4. The end of the completed bias tube after it's been drawn out of the cylinder, shown here still attached to the metal wire.

5. To make a flower, coil the end of the tube in the center, make five small loop petals around the coil, then tack the loops down with Nymo beading thread. To make a large petal, fold 6 inches (15.2 cm) of tube in half, tack each end underneath the center of the flower, then pinch and tack down the loop with tiny stitches.

6. A completed bias-tube fantasy flower layered with Japanese ribbon stitches and accented with purple glass beads.

BIAS-TUBE FLOWERS

Long bias tubes can be used to create a variety of elaborate flowers. In the example shown in the step-by-step sequence, I used 12 inches (30.5 cm) of hand-dyed silk charmeuse that I had bias-cut into $1/4$-inch-wide (0.6 cm) ribbons (see page 15 for instructions).

To expedite the task of turning a long bias tube inside out after its seam has been stitched closed, I use a simple tool called the Fasturn, which consists of a long metal cylinder and a hooked wire. The wire is inserted into the cylinder and hooked through the end of the bias tube; when the wire is pulled out of the cylinder, it takes the tube up through the cylinder and turns it inside out.

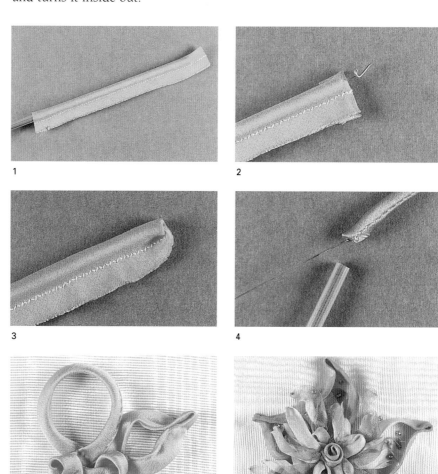

1

2

3

4

5

6

BERRIES

1. Cut a circle out of ribbon or fabric. About 1/8 inch (0.3 cm) from the edge, stitch small running stitches of Nymo beading thread around the circumference of the circle. Gently pull on the thread to gather the circle, but do not close it.

2. Stuff the berry with polyester fiberfill, pull the thread tightly to gather the circle closed, then knot off the thread. If the ribbon or fabric is thick, it may be necessary to secure the gathers by taking several additional stitches across the opening. The berry shown at right is ready to be stitched to fabric.

3. To segment the berry, bring the thread up through its center, then take the thread around the side and up through the center again, pulling tightly. Repeat to create several segments of equal size, then knot off the thread on the back.

4. The strawberries in this arrangement were made with 32mm white silk ribbon painted with Pêbēo Setasilk silk paint in red. To make the large strawberry, a circle was stuffed to make a cone shape, then embellished with brown Delica beads.

Berries, which are stuffed circles of ribbon or fabric, are fun to make. Instead of a tube, a circle of ribbon or fabric is the initial form for this motif. When cutting, remember that the diameter of the initial circle of ribbon or fabric should be twice that of the completed berry. In the example below, I cut a circle 2 inches (5 cm) in diameter from 2-inch-wide burgundy velvet ribbon, which gave me a berry approximately 1 inch (2.5 cm) in diameter.

A berry can also be segmented to serve as the center of a stitched flower. In the elaborate flower shown below, the berry was "quilted" into sections with gold thread, then surrounded with two rows of Japanese ribbon stitch petals in 9mm gold organdy with metallic edging.

1

3

2

4

DAFFODIL

STITCHES
Stem stitch
Japanese ribbon stitch

MATERIALS
Fabric
6-inch (15.2-cm) square of ivory moiré
Silk Ribbon
16 inches (40.6 cm)
13 mm hand-dyed yellow
7mm green
8 inches (20.3 cm)
13mm hand-dyed orange
Thread and Floss
1 skein green rayon floss
Nymo beading thread

1. Stitch Japanese ribbon stitch petals with the yellow ribbon.
2. Following the instructions on page 88, construct a small tube from the orange silk ribbon, then stitch it in the center of the yellow petals with Nymo thread. Make sure the seam of the tube is positioned toward the fabric so that it will not be visible.
3. Stem stitch the stems with green rayon floss.
4. Add Japanese ribbon stitch leaves in green ribbon.

The completed daffodil.

IRIS

STITCHES
Japanese ribbon stitch
Straight stitch

MATERIALS

Fabric
8-inch (20.3-cm) square
of green moiré silk

Silk Ribbon
12 inches (30.5 cm)
13mm hand-dyed lilac
13mm hand-dyed
green variegated
13mm hand-dyed
purple
4 inches (10.2 cm)
*¹⁄₂-inch (1.3 cm) bias-cut
yellow*

Thread and Floss
1 skein Kelly green
rayon floss
Nymo beading thread

1. Stitch the central petals of the iris with two side-by-side Japanese ribbon stitches in lilac ribbon.
2. Complete the iris with four Japanese ribbon stitch petals in purple ribbon, making two loose horizontal stitches on the sides of the lilac stitches, and two vertical stitches immediately below them.
3. Following the instructions on page 82, use the Nymo thread to gather three 1-inch-long (2.5 cm) pieces of yellow bias-cut ribbon. Fray the edges, then tack one of the gathered ribbons in the middle of the four vertical petals, and one between each of the lateral petals and the central lilac petals. This creates the beard of the iris.
4. Use the green ribbon to add two long Japanese ribbon stitch leaves.
5. To make a bud, stitch one straight stitch with lilac ribbon, then stitch a small Japanese ribbon stitch on either side with green ribbon.
6. Stem stitch the stems with three strands of Kelly green floss.

The completed iris.

DAY LILY

STITCHES

Straight stitch

Japanese ribbon stitch

Twisted Japanese ribbon stitch

MATERIALS

Fabric

8-inch (20.3-cm) square of green moiré silk

Ribbon

24 inches (60.9 cm) 13mm hand-dyed coral-and-orange silk

4 inches (10.2 cm) 1/2-inch-wide (1.3 cm) hand-dyed pale brown bias-cut silk

1 card 9mm forest green Mokuba rayon

Thread and Floss

1 skein forest green rayon floss

1 skein coral rayon floss

Nymo beading thread

Embellishments

30 brown Delica glass beads

Miscellaneous

Brown Zig textile marker

1. Stitch the central part of the lily with short Japanese ribbon stitches in coral-and-orange ribbon, three pointing upward and three downward.
2. Add three long, loose twisted Japanese ribbon stitches to the bottom.
3. Extend four loose straight stitch pistils in coral floss down from the center.
4. To make a lily bud, use the pale brown bias-cut ribbon to stitch two side-by-side straight stitches.
5. Stem stitch the stems with three strands of green floss.
6. Add small Japanese ribbon stitch leaves at the base of the stems with green tape.
7. To create the stigma, use the Nymo thread to stitch several beads at the end of each pistil.
8. Lightly touch the nib of the brown textile marker to each of the lily's petals several times. Note that in some cases the ink will bleed slightly, creating small starlike shapes, a common effect on silk.

The completed day lily.

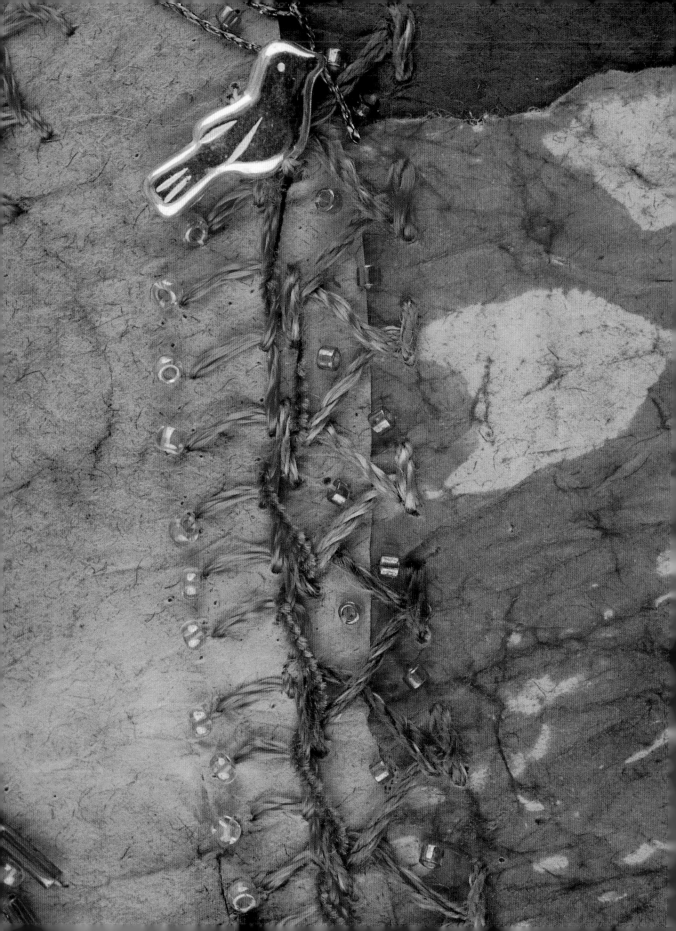

CRAZY QUILT STITCHES AND APPLIQUÉ

(Opposite) A detail
of a handmade fan
was made from
decoratively cut and
torn handmade
marbleized papers
that were appliquéd
to a muslin ground
with Nymo thread,
then embellished
with a variety of
crazy quilt stitches,
beads, and charms.
(Right) Bond America
"Multis" variegated
rayon threads were
used to stitch these
crazy quilt stitches.

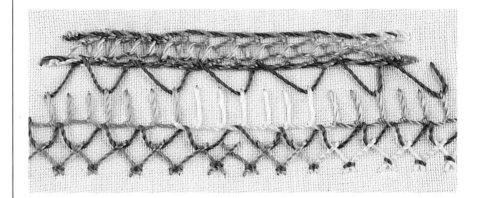

This chapter covers two traditional embroidery and fabric embellishment techniques—crazy quilt stitching and appliqué—and seeks to demystify and simplify both. Crazy quilts were first made by Victorian matrons whose wealth and leisure enabled them to profusely embellish their quilts, which consisted of patches of ornate fabrics, laces, trims, and personal mementos. The elaborate embroidery stitches they devised to define the edges of each quilt patch are combinations of basic stitches. Appliqué—the process of applying fabric cutouts to another piece of fabric—is the perfect showcase for crazy quilt stitches, and three very basic appliqué techniques are shown in this chapter: simple straight stitch appliqué, appliqué using fusible webbing, and appliqué using acid-free appliqué paper.

CRAZY QUILT STITCHES

The stitches in this part of the book are arranged according to degree of difficulty, from easiest to most difficult. Many of the basic stitches demonstrated on pages 48–57 provide the foundation for more elaborate crazy quilt stitches. For example, the maidenhair stitch (see page 99) is a variation on the feather stitch (page 55), and the lazy daisy (page 54) serves as the basis for the whipped chain stitch (page 99).

To create imaginative, eye-catching borders, crazy quilt stitches should be combined and superimposed. These stitches are traditionally worked in thread, floss, and yarn, but could be worked just as easily in narrow widths of ribbon.

QUILTER'S KNOT
A quilter's knot prepares your thread or floss for the stress of repetitive stitching.

1. Thread the needle, then wrap the thread around the barrel of the needle twice.

2. Place your thumb over the wrapped thread. Holding the thread tightly, slide it down the barrel of the needle, over the eye, and down to the end of the thread.

3. The completed quilter's knot.

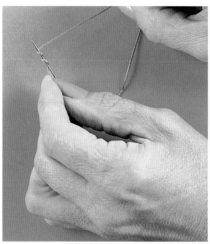

1

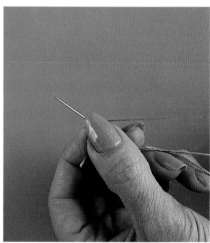

2

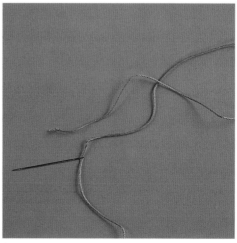

3

BUTTONHOLE OR BLANKET STITCH

This extremely common stitch, which is worked from left to right, can be seen on many quilts and folk-art embroidery designs.

1. Bring the thread through to the front of the fabric at A. Making a diagonal straight stitch, go down at B, then re-emerge at C.

2. Reinsert the needle through the fabric at D and re-emerge at E— points parallel to B and C in step 1—aligning the thread under the tip of the needle. Pull the needle through until the stitch is snug against the fabric. To avoid puckering or distorting the fabric, do not pull the thread too tightly. Repeat this step to extend the line of stitches.

3. Completed blanket or buttonhole stitches. To finish a line of stitches, take the needle through over the thread at the corner of the last stitch, then tie off the thread on the back of the fabric.

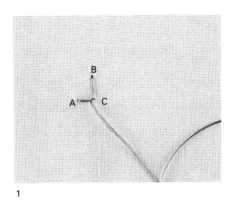

1

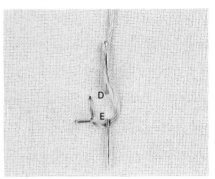

2

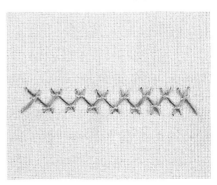

3

HERRINGBONE STITCH

This variation on the cross stitch is also worked from left to right. For your first few tries, draw two parallel guidelines on the fabric approximately ½ inch (1.3 cm) apart with a fade-away or water-soluble fabric marking pen.

1. To begin, bring the needle up through the fabric at A and go back down at B to make a diagonal stitch. Emerge at C, then cross over the first stitch and go down at D. Come back up at E, make a small backstitch at F. To cross over the resulting diagonal stitch, go back down at a point parallel to D. Repeat.

2. Completed herringbone stitches, embellished at intersecting threads with straight stitches.

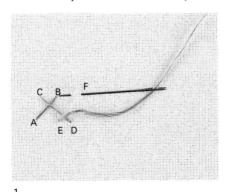

1

2

1. Bring the needle up through the fabric at A and go down at B to make a horizontal straight stitch. Come back up at C (near the center of the stitch), then take a diagonal straight stitch by going back down at D. Make another horizontal stitch by taking the needle into the fabric and emerging at E. Take another diagonal straight stitch to make a V shape and repeat, alternating from side to side.

2. Completed chevron stitches.

1. To begin, take a diagonal straight stitch by coming up through the fabric at A and going down at B. Come back up at C (about one-fifth of the way from the bottom of the first stitch) and take the thread over the first stitch. Insert the needle into the fabric at D and emerge at E, again with the needle over the thread. This horizontal stitch will pull the diagonal thread into a curve.

2. Continue making evenly spaced vertical stitches, alternating between the top and bottom of the row and always working the needle over the thread.

3. Completed Cretan stitches.

CHEVRON STITCH

The chevron stitch is worked from left to right. As with the herringbone stitch (see page 97), beginning stitchers should draw two parallel guidelines about ½ inch (1.3 cm) apart directly on the fabric with a fade-away or water-soluble fabric marking pen.

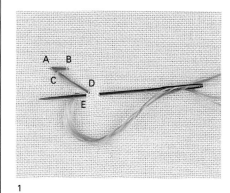

1

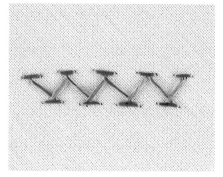

2

CRETAN STITCH

This ornamental loop stitch is worked from left to right. With practice, you'll be able to space your stitches evenly.

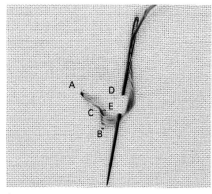

1

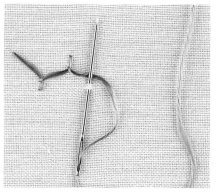

2

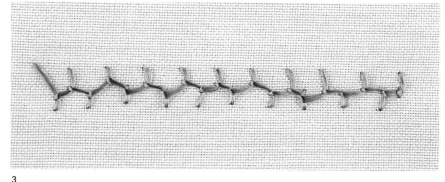

3

1. Come up at point A, then go down at B and come back up at C. Working to the left of the Y, go down at D (a point parallel to A) and come back up at E (aligned directly below C). To complete a third branch, which should be slightly longer than the second, go down at F and come up at G (aligned with C and E). Repeat by working stitches to the right.

2. Completed maidenhair stitches.

1. To begin the chain, make a lazy daisy, but instead of finishing it with an anchor stitch, loop the thread again, then insert the needle through the fabric so that it passes *under* the loop of the preceding stitch and emerges to create another loop. Repeat to stitch a chain, then stitch a second, parallel chain.

2. Bring the needle through the fabric near the first loop of one of the chains, pass the thread through the outside part of each loop, then go back down at the end of the chain. (The needle should pierce the fabric *only* at the beginning and end of the chain.)

3. The stitch is completed by using a third color to whip the two chains together. Starting at the tops of the chains, take the needle through one loop, then the other immediately opposite. Repeat for the entire length of the chain.

MAIDENHAIR STITCH

The maidenhair stitch is actually a series of feather stitches (see page 54), except that one branch of each Y shape lengthens slightly with each stitch.

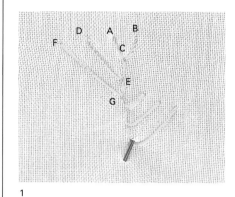

1

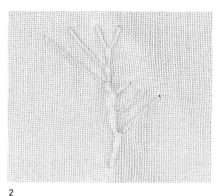

2

WHIPPED CHAIN STITCH

In this crazy quilt stitch, two lines of parallel chain stitches—actually a continuous series of lazy daisies (see page 54)—are joined together by "whipping" thread through the loops of the chains.

1

2

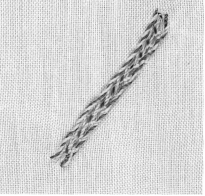

3

99

APPLIQUÉ

The term "appliqué" is derived from a French word, *appliquer,* which means "to apply" or "to lay on." An excellent companion for embroidery, appliqué is used in this book to create a the bodies of a toucan (see page 67), a fish (page 70), and a seagoat (page 72), and to embellish a blouse (page 128) and a wall hanging (page 134).

In traditional forms of appliqué, a piece of fabric is cut out so that its grain lines will align with those of the fabric ground, the edges of the cutout are turned under and clipped into V shapes so they will lie flat, and the cutout is covertly stitched to the fabric with blind stitches that are hidden beneath its edges—a time-consuming process. This section reviews three quick and easy appliqué methods that are accessible even to beginning stitchers.

SIMPLE STRAIGHT STITCH APPLIQUÉ

In this method, a piece of ribbon is appliquéd around its perimeter with small straight stitches using floss or thread and an embroidery needle. There is no need to align the grain lines of the ribbon and the fabric ground, and no attempt is made to hide the stitching, which can be done in a color that either matches or contrasts with that of the cutout. In the example below, the colors of the thread and the appliquéd ribbon are so similar that the stitches can be discerned only on very close observation, so that the shape appears to float above the fabric. If desired, the edges of the cutout can be embellished with couching (see page 50) or crazy quilt stitches (see pages 97–99). This appliqué technique was used on the blouse project on page 128.

This piece of painted silk ribbon, which was burned into an abstract shape, was straight-stitched around its perimeter to an ivory silk moiré ground with two strands of pink silk floss.

FUSIBLE WEBBING

Another easy method of appliqué uses iron-on fusible webbing, which bonds a cutout to fabric without stitching. In addition to the fusible webbing, which can be purchased at fabric stores, you'll need a standard household steam iron and a press cloth or towel. This method works best with fabrics whose edges are unlikely to ravel, such as the Ultrasuede used in the demonstration below.

To make a precise shape like the star that's shown in the demonstration below, cut a template from a piece of cardboard, then use the template to cut out the shape from your fabric with a pair of sharp scissors.

1. Trace the outline of the appliqué shape on the fabric with a fade-away or water-soluble fabric pen. Fill an iron with water, then preheat it on the "cotton" setting. Cut a piece of the webbing that's slightly larger than the appliqué fabric.

2. Peel off the release paper from the fusible webbing and place the traced fabric on it. Cover the fabric with a damp press cloth or towel and, working one small area at a time, press firmly with the iron for about 10 seconds while applying continuous steam.

3. Cut the appliqué shape out of the fused fabric. Peel off the white paper backing, position the shape on the fabric ground, and repeat the ironing instructions noted in step 2 to bond it to the ground.

4. The edges of the appliquéd shape are finished here with buttonhole stitches stitched with a rayon thread variegated in red, blue, and yellow.

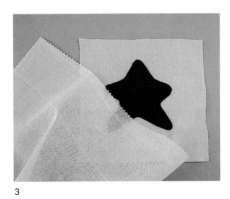

1

2

3

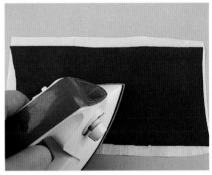

4

APPLIQUÉ PAPER AND FUSIBLE WEBBING TAPE

Like the fusible webbing method described on page 101, appliqué done with acid-free appliqué paper and ¹/₄-inch-wide (0.6 cm) fusible webbing involves bonding the appliqué shape to a fabric ground with a hot, steaming iron. This method is particularly suited to appliqué cutouts with raw, rough edges.

A couple of important product notes: Kate's Appliqué Paper, the only acid-free appliqué paper on the market, will not break down and deteriorate fabrics; and Steam-A-Seam fusible webbing is pliable enough to be pierced with a needle, an important feature when decorative stitching is desired.

In the example below, silk ties were dismantled, immersion-dyed in burgundy, and cut into star shapes (using a cardboard template) before they were fused with the appliqué paper and webbing tape. To see these stars in a completed mixed-media composition, turn to page 134.

1. Using a fade-away or water-soluble marking pen, trace the template on the fabric, then cut out the shape, leaving about ¹/₄ inch (0.6 cm) around its outline. Trace the template on a piece of appliqué paper and cut it out, this time following its traced outline exactly. Pin the paper shape to the wrong side of the fabric, then remove the backing from the fusible webbing tape and apply it to the perimeter of the paper shape. Notch the seam allowance so it will lie flat, then remove the second backing from the tape and fold the seams down over it.

2. Remove the pins from the fabric. Using a damp press cloth or towel to protect the fabric, iron both sides of the shape to fuse it to the tape. These star shapes are ready to be stitched to a fabric ground.

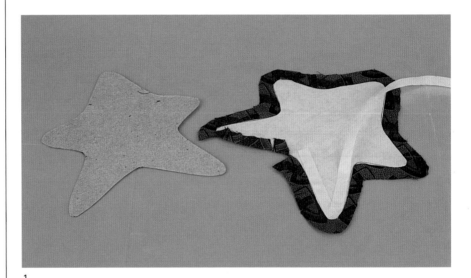

1

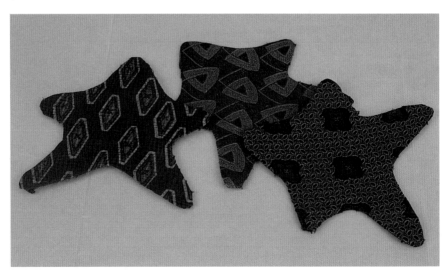

2

APPLIQUÉ AND FABRIC STABILIZERS

Vintage and extremely delicate fabrics and laces can be difficult to handle, especially when attempting to appliqué them or embellish them with stitching or beads. These materials tend to have little or no body, often pucker when pinned or basted to fabrics, and could be damaged if mounted on an embroidery hoop or a Q-Snap. To avoid these problems, I apply a water-soluble fabric stabilizer such as PerfectSew (see the source directory), which is nontoxic, dries quickly, and can be applied to a variety of fibers, including the most fragile fabrics. This product seals frayed edges and stiffens fabric so that it doesn't need to be mounted on a hoop and can be pinned and/or basted easily.

1. When I found a 50-year-old piece of champagne-colored lace in a sample book, I decided that it would look exquisite appliquéd on an ivory moiré silk ground. I brushed the entire piece with fabric stabilizer (including its slightly ragged edges); once dry, the lace was ready for stitching.

2. The appliquéd and embellished vintage lace. I began by basting the lace to the fabric with champagne-colored Nymo beading thread. I stitched small Japanese ribbon stitches within the outlines of the flowers and leaves, using 4mm silk ribbon in the same color as the lace so as not to detract from its elegant design. As a finishing touch, I outlined the perimeter of the lace and the stems within its design with pale champagne Delica beads.

1

2

WORKING WITH CRAFT MEDIA

(Opposite) A detail
of a composition
(see page 109) that
features stenciling,
fabric markers,
ribbon embroidery,
beads, and buttons.
(Right) The white
areas of this silk tie
were treated with a
water-soluble resist
before being painted
(see page 113).

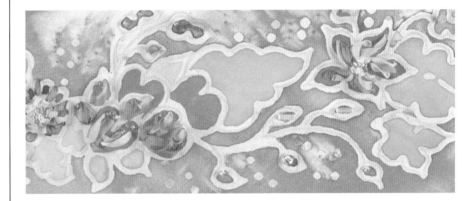

If a preoccupation with needlecrafts has kept you from exploring the joys of other crafts, stop putting off the inevitable and take the time to explore your creative potential.

This chapter examines a variety of popular media that can be used to enhance ribbon embroidery. Stamps and stencils, whether commercially produced, handmade, or "found," can serve either as stitch patterns or as integral elements of a ribbon embroidery composition. In addition, two methods for painting fabric grounds—the ancient technique of silk painting and the fine-art medium of watercolor—are explained. Polymer clay, a plastic-based material that is cured at low temperatures in a home oven, is used to make embellishments that heighten the depth and dimension of embroidery. The tools required for these techniques are easy to use and can be found at most hobby, craft, and art supply stores.

STAMPING

Stamping can be a truly creative medium, with applications that extend far beyond paper. By using the appropriate inks or paints, a stamp can transform a dull, plain fabric into one invigorated with color and texture, either with a single print or a complex pattern.

Before you begin, wash the fabric in a mild detergent, let air dry, then press it to straighten the grain. Use only inks, pads, and markers that are specially formulated for use with fabrics. Since most fabric inks must be heat-set on the reverse side, usually with an iron or hair dryer at a high setting, sturdy, natural-fiber and natural-fiber/synthetic blend fabrics are your best choices.

RUBBER STAMPS

A rubber stamp is a wise and economical addition to your sewing box. A single rubber stamp print creates an instant ribbon embroidery pattern. As shown in the project on pages 122–123, large-scale stamps can provide a background for embroidered details.

Ink can be applied to a rubber stamp in several ways. If you're using a stamp pad, gently tap the stamp die on the pad. If you're using a bottled ink, just tap its dabber on the die. In addition to coloring in a stamped print, markers can be used to ink a stamp directly. In any case, make sure that the entire surface of the die is covered, but avoid over-inking it or a smudged print is the likely result.

To make a print, place the inked die on the fabric and apply firm and even pressure to the stamp. (Do *not* rock the stamp back and forth.) Remove the stamp and let the print dry. You can correct any missed areas with a fabric marker in a matching color. If desired, color in part or all of the print with fabric markers. Heat-set the inks as directed by the manufacturer, then embellish with stitching.

The swan stamp at left was used as a pattern for ribbon embroidery stitches on a heart-shaped ornament.

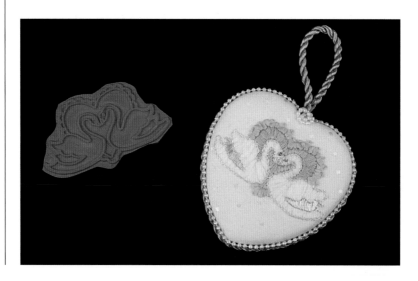

CARVED STAMPS

If you'd like to stamp fabric with an original large-scale image that has a minimum of detail, you can make your own by cutting up a pop-up sponge or by carving an art gum eraser.

- *Sponge Stamps.* Draw a shape on the dry pop-up sponge with a pencil, then cut around its outline with a craft knife. Submerge the sponge shape in water, then wring it out well until it is lightly damp.
- *Eraser Stamps.* Draw a shape on a small end of an art gum eraser with a pencil. Use a craft knife to carve away the areas of the eraser surrounding the shape, so that the shape stands away in relief from the rest of the eraser.

To achieve smooth, even prints, these stamps must be inked with a 1-inch-wide (2.5 cm) foam brayer. Use an old plastic spoon to transfer a small amount of fabric ink or paint to a Styrofoam tray or plate. Load the brayer with ink or paint, then use the brayer to apply the medium to the stamp.

In the demonstration below, I used Lumiere fabric paint (see page 23), which gave the prints a sparkling, opaque finish. Since this paint dries quickly and is permanent, it was necessary for me to set up a cleaning station, where soiled stamps and other tools could be placed so that the paint would dissolve before it had a chance to dry. To make a cleaning station, place a dampened household foam sponge into a deep plastic tray, then fill the tray with enough household cleaner that contains ammonia (such as Formula 409) to cover the sponge. Once a stamp or tool has been soiled with paint, dip it into the cleaner and wipe it off on the sponge.

1. Use a sponge brayer to apply inks and paints to sponge and eraser stamps.

2. For clean, clear prints, make sure the medium is uniformly applied.

3. Exert consistent pressure on the stamp when making a print.

4. Once the prints are dry, they can be embellished with stitching. In this example, a sponge print has been outlined with gold beads and straight stitches in 4mm gold silk ribbon, and an eraser print has been finished with gold metallic thread and gold beads.

1

2

3

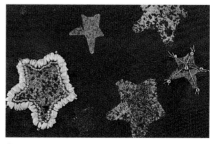

4

"NATURAL" STAMPS

Just about any flat object with a nonabsorbent surface can be used to stamp a print. To make the example shown below, I created a stamp by drying a maple leaf for several months in a flower press. I used a foam brayer to load the dried leaf with Lumiere fabric paint (see page 23), placed it inked side down on a piece of midnight blue Ultrasuede, then printed it by gently rolling it with a rolling pin. After it had dried, I embellished the print with ribbon, threads, and beads.

Two maple leaves—one fresh, one dried and inked with paint—and a completed leaf print.

The leaf print embellished with Japanese ribbon stitches in 4mm handpainted silk ribbons along bronze and gold metallic braid veins. Additional veins are stitched with petite metallic beads.

STENCILING

Stenciling—applying paint into the open areas, or *windows*, of a material that can effectively mask the surface beneath—is another craft that can be integrated with ribbon embroidery. In addition to purchasing precut stencils, you can make stencils prints with some very ordinary—and unexpected—household items.

As when stamping, you'll need to wash, dry, and press the fabric beforehand, and always stencil with paints specially formulated for use with fabrics. I also used double-ended fabric markers fitted with a fine point and a brush to add grass, a meandering vine, and a cobblestone path to my stenciled scene.

PRECUT STENCILS

Available in a wide range of styles, designs, and sizes, precut stencils are usually made from paper, transparent plastic film, and metal (such as the door stencil shown below). You'll also need masking tape, a Styrofoam plate, paper toweling, and a small stencil brush. To ensure an even load and prevent paint from bleeding beneath the stencil, wrap the stencil brush bristles tightly with masking tape.

1. Position the stencil on the fabric, then secure it with two small pieces of masking tape. Place a small amount of paint on the plate, lightly load the stencil brush, then remove most of the paint by blotting the brush on a paper towel. Using a light pouncing motion, apply the paint within the stencil windows.

2. Once the stencil print had dried, draw details freehand with fabric markers. Heat-set the paints and markers as indicated in the manufacturers' instructions.

3. The completed stenciled door, embellished with French knots, Japanese ribbon stitches, gold glass beads, and ceramic animal buttons. The muslin ground was dyed using the plastic bag technique (see page 29). Brass stencil by American Traditional Stencils.

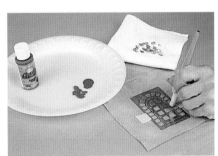

1

2

3

"FOUND" STENCILS

You may never have thought about it, but there are many items around the house that can serve as stencils. If you have paper doilies left over from your last holiday gathering, you can get started right away. For the demonstration below, I created a stencil by cutting a corner out of a large rectangular doily. To ensure a smooth, clean print, I used a foam roller instead of a stencil brush. The Lumiere fabric paint (see page 23) required that I set up a cleaning station (see page 107).

1. Affix the doily to the fabric by spraying a light coat of repositionable spray adhesive to the back.

2. Load the foam roller evenly with paint, then roll it over the doily. Let dry, then heat-set if necessary.

3. The completed print.

4. Here, the doily print has been embroidered with spider web roses, lazy daisies, French knots, and twisted Japanese ribbon stitches.

1

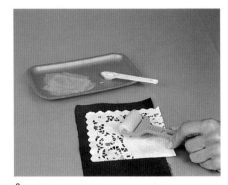

2

3

4

WATERCOLOR

The traditional painting support for transparent watercolor—one of the most popular fine-art media in the world—is high-quality white paper. In order to combine watercolor with embroidery, I used raw cotton painter's canvas (usually called cotton duck), which can be purchased at art supply or fabric stores. With its highly visible warp and weft, raw cotton canvas is similar in appearance to aida cloth, making it excellent for stitching as well as painting. Unlike cotton fabrics sold in fabric stores, it is unnecessary to wash cotton canvas in preparation for painting because it is not treated with any chemicals.

If this is your first experience with watercolor, you should buy just a limited number of colors—ten at most—in small tubes. I prefer Winsor & Newton transparent watercolors; to achieve a similar effect, you can use artists' acrylic paints that have been thinned with water. You'll also need a pencil, a liner brush, a small plastic palette with paint wells, and a container of water.

Begin by sketching in pencil directly on the canvas. To achieve depth and dimension, apply several thin washes. Once the paint has dried, the composition can be embellished with silk ribbon.

SILK PAINTING

Silk painting is defined as the application of dyes to silk fabric. There are two principal approaches to this craft. One produces abstract, painterly effects; variations on this approach can be used to paint ribbon (see pages 30–35). The other, which is more widely used by professional silk painters and surface designers, employs a clear water-soluble resist; this technique is usually used to create representational images.

As with most other fabric painting techniques, you'll need to wash the silk in a mild soap-and-water solution before you begin. If you intend to paint in a loose style, damp silk will enhance the effect. Otherwise, let the silk air-dry completely, then proceed.

Before you start, read "Working with Dyes and Paints," pages 17–20. Cover your worksurface, organize all your materials, put on old clothes, and wear plastic gloves.

THE PAINTERLY TECHNIQUE

For the demonstration below, I painted a damp silk scarf with Jacquard Silk Colors dyes in red, yellow, and blue. I placed a small amount of each dye in the well of a plastic palette and used one Chinese calligraphy brush for each color. I scrunched the scarf because I wanted the colors to run into its wrinkles and folds, but it could have been placed flat or even stretched (see page 126). The wet dye can then be treated with salt or alcohol. Let dry for 24 hours, then heat-set the dye according to the manufacturer's instructions.

1. Using a separate brush for each color, apply the dyes to the scarf. Working quickly, apply colors right next to each other so they will run together.

2. While the dyes are still wet, you can add texture by sprinkling the silk with salt. Let dry for 24 hours, then heat-set as directed.

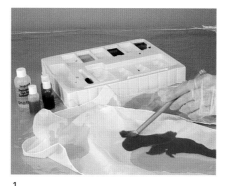

1

2

WORKING WITH A WATER-SOLUBLE RESIST

Resists, which are used to control and contain the flow of dyes, are typically applied to silk with a small plastic squeeze bottle fitted with a metal applicator tip. To achieve lines of consistent weight, pressure must be applied to the bottle continuously. Because my hands fatigue easily, I use the AirPen applicator (available through Silkpaint Corporation, Inc; see source directory), which eliminates hand fatigue and makes clean, straight, continuous lines without blobbing. The AirPen can also be used with paints, dyes, glues, and Fiber-Etch gel (see page 131).

Because the resist spreads slightly as it is applied, tightly rendered, complex designs should be avoided. The preferable method of pattern transfer is to lay a pattern underneath the stretched silk and trace it with resist. When multiple layers of fabric or opacity do not permit tracing, such as the tie shown below, you can sketch your design in pencil, but you must work carefully because pencil cannot be erased from silk. (Do not use fade-away or water-soluble marking pens for your drawing, as they may be set into the fabric by the resist.)

Apply the resist, then let dry. Working within the resist lines, use a small brush to apply each dye color to the fabric. The dye will flow and fill the fabric, stopping at the resist. After the painting is completed and the dyes are still wet, apply salt or alcohol if desired. Let dry, then heat-set the dyes following the manufacturer's instructions.

1. Applying resist to a silk tie with the AirPen. The flow of resist is controlled by covering the airhole on the applicator with your finger. To reduce vibration, I placed the air compressor on a foam mouse pad. Silk tie blank from Rupert, Gibbon & Spider.

2. A silk-painted tie embellished with Japanese ribbon stitches, French knots, and beads. To add the embroidery, I snipped open the threads of the lining on the back of the tie; to conceal the back of the ribbonwork, I whip-stitched the seam closed.

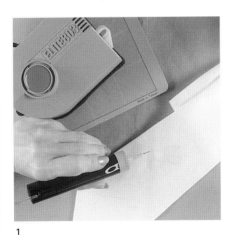

1

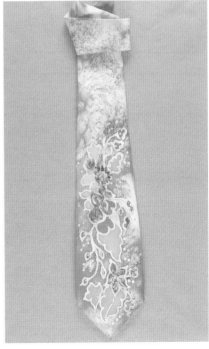

2

POLYMER CLAY EMBELLISHMENTS

Instead of having to search for the "perfect" embellishments for a project, you can make your own with polymer clay. Although polymer clay behaves much like traditional earth-based clays, it's actually composed of particles of polyvinyl chloride (PVC) suspended in a plasticizer. Available in wide range of colors, polymer clay is soft and moldable at room temperature, and can be carved, stamped, drilled, painted, and sanded. Instead of firing it in a high-temperature kiln, polymer clay is baked (properly referred to as "cured") in a standard home-use oven or toaster oven at approximately 250°F, which fuses the PVC particles into a hard, durable plastic.

Polymer clay can be purchased at craft, hobby, and art supply stores. The most widely available brands are Sculpey, Fimo, and Cernit. For the demonstration, I used white Sculpey to make a small egg that I stamped with a floral design. Part of the fun of working with polymer clay is improvising with tools; for example, I used a Pyrex casserole lid as a working and curing surface, and a rolling pin to roll out the clay. (Note: Once you've used a kitchen item with polymer clay, NEVER use it to prepare food.) You'll also need a piece of cardboard (to make a template), a craft knife, a rubber stamp, textile markers, a piece of white paper, an oven or toaster oven (to cure the clay), a spray glaze such as FolkArt Spray Clearcote Hi-Shine Brilliant Glaze by Plaid Enterprises (to seal the stamped image), and a strong, permanent adhesive such as E6000 (to affix the embellishment to the fabric).

To cure the clay, bake it on an oven-safe surface at about 250°F for 15 to 20 minutes (follow the package instructions). Let cool; without touching the stamp print, transfer the shape to a piece of newspaper or paper toweling, then seal the print with a coat of the spray glaze. (Work in a well-ventilated room.) Let dry, then spray the entire shape with a second coat.

1. Knead a small piece of the clay for a few minutes, then roll it out to an $1/8$ inch (0.3 cm) thick.

2. Place the cardboard template on top of the clay and cut around its perimeter with the craft knife. Carefully remove the excess clay from around the shape.

3. Ink the rubber stamp with a textile marker, then make a test print on a piece of paper.

4. Re-ink the stamp, exhale on the die through your mouth to reactivate the ink, then stamp the clay shape without rocking the stamp. Cure the clay as directed, let cool, then finish with two coats of spray glaze.

5. To incorporate the shape into a stitch design, place it on the fabric ground, trace its outline with a water-soluble pen, then set it aside. If desired, use Zig textile markers to draw some details, then heat-set. Embellish the composition with embroidery stitches, then glue the shape in place.

1

2

3

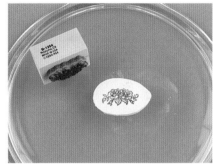

4

5

BRINGING IT ALL TOGETHER

(Opposite) The completed étui project (see page 124). (Right) A detail from the rubber-stamped portraits project (page 122).

The nine projects in this chapter juxtapose and combine most of the painting, dyeing, stitching, and craft techniques demonstrated in this book. The finished pieces are not intended to serve as models, nor should the accompanying text be followed to the letter. On the contrary, I created these projects to show how an abundance of materials and media can be imaginatively and elegantly integrated to create unique wearables, gifts, and heirlooms; to provide readers with inspiration and direction; and to demonstrate silk ribbon's boundless versatility.

RIBBON-EMBROIDERED BLOUSE

STITCHES
Japanese ribbon stitch
Spider web rose
Plume stitch
French knot loop stitch
See also pages 48–57

MATERIALS
Project
Brown silk blouse
Ribbons
Handpainted and -dyed standard and bias-cut silk in a range of widths
Embellishments
4mm pearls

This project shows how hand-dyed and handpainted ribbons, both standard and bias-cut in a range of widths, can enhance a purchased blouse beautifully. I used several simple embroidery stitches—mainly the loop stitch, Japanese ribbon stitch, and spider web rose—to create a freeform floral design on the collar and the French-style cuffs. The frayed edges of the bias-cut-ribbon Japanese ribbon stitches and spider web roses contrast gently with the stitches made with standard ribbon and the pearl embellishments.

HEAT-STAMPED VELVET VEST

Heat-stamping is an exciting, fun way to embellish velvet fabrics. By misting the back of the velvet with water, placing the damp fabric nap side down on a hard red rubber stamp die, then ironing the damp area with a very hot, dry iron, you can "carve" stamp prints into the fabric. Note that the stamp *must* be made with hard red rubber or it won't be able to withstand the heat of the iron, so foam stamps are not appropriate for this technique. Also, the stamp die must have high reliefs in order to make an impression in the nap; though few images are deeply cut enough for this application, a wide variety of stamps can be obtained from Hot Potatoes (see source directory).

HEAT-STAMPING THE VELVET

The fabric I used to make the vest is a rayon/silk velvet available from Rupert, Gibbon & Spider. (For more dramatic prints, use a rayon/acetate velvet.) Following the package instructions, I immersion-dyed the velvet with Dylon Cold Water Dye in Mexican red. I pinned the pattern pieces of the vest to the back of the dyed fabric, outlined them with a water-soluble fabric marker (dressmaker's chalk can also be used), then removed them to make the heat prints. I placed the rubber stamp die side up on a hard, flat surface, laid the velvet nap side down over the die, then I misted the area of the velvet positioned over the die with water. Using a dry iron set on the "wool" setting, I ironed the misted area while counting to 20. I repeated the process to stamp the nap randomly, but made prints only on areas of the vest that would be unaffected by seams.

STITCHING

Using a variety of stitches, I embroidered the teacup prints on the front of the vest only with 4mm silk ribbon, stitching small arrangements by the handles, near the saucers, or at the tops of the cups, then added small gold Delica beads, bugle beads, and glass beads.

MAKING THE VEST

I cut the fabric following the traced outlines of the pattern, then used the pattern to cut a lining from matching red taffeta.

Because its nap shifts incessantly, velvet is a very difficult fabric to stitch, which accounts, in part, for the high cost of velvet clothing. To achieve optimal results, baste a perforated tear-away stabilizer to the back of the velvet, and use a suit interlining when sewing the lining to the inside of the vest. Also, after testing several brands of red cotton thread, I found that only Tire red silk buttonhole twist could be used to stitch the velvet. Note that washing and ironing heat-stamped velvet will remove the prints, but dry cleaning does not have this effect.

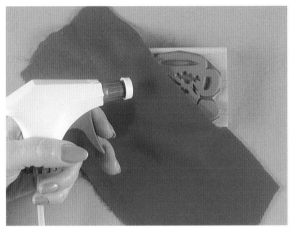

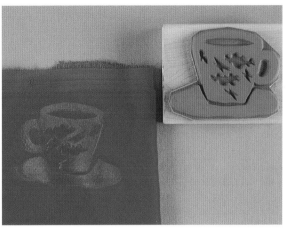

Place the velvet nap side down on the rubber die and mist the back of the velvet with water. To "carve" the print into the nap, apply a hot iron to the dampened area for 10 to 20 seconds.

A completed heat-stamped print.

(Left) The completed heat-stamped velvet vest, and a detail of a heat-stamped teacup print embellished with ribbon embroidery (right).

STAMP PRINT PORTRAITS

This framed composition features stamp prints of three Edwardian ladies embellished with fabric markers and ribbon embroidery. Such large-scale stamps would work equally well as individual framed portraits (to make a charming wall grouping) or as quilt blocks. Brown ink gave the prints a vintage look.

STAMPING AND COLORING

After I washed, dried, and pressed the silk broadcloth, I taped it to my worktable, stretching it as tightly as I could without distorting the fabric. (For maximum tension, the fabric can also be mounted on an embroidery hoop or a Q-Snap.) I marked a stamp positioning guideline across the bottom of the fabric with a water-soluble fabric marker.

I carefully loaded the stamp die with ink by dabbing its surface with the brown stamping ink, making sure the entire die was coated. Since working with large stamps requires some practice, I made several test prints before stamping the fabric. Once I was ready, I loaded the die once more, then stamped the fabric, pressing down evenly on the wood mount. When necessary, I used a marker in a matching color to fill in any weak areas.

Once the ink had dried completely, I filled in selected areas with blendable, dual-ended fabric markers in a variety of colors. As with the stamp inks, I tested the fabric markers before using them to color the prints, as many brands have a tendency to bleed. I filled in the borders with green, each lady's face with peach, and used a few other colors on some of the clothing and hats. I worked with a light touch, as dark spots often result when a marker tip is left on the fabric for too long. I let the markers dry, then heat-set the inks as directed.

STITCHING

I began by stitching the hair. In the lefthand portrait, I couched Mokuba silver bouclé ribbon to simulate a permanent wave; in the center and righthand portraits, I stitched variegated silk ribbon in double-wrap French knots.

For the hat in the lefthand portrait, I used 13mm variegated bias-cut ribbon to make a simple gathered flower and "feathers," then added two loops on either side of the lady's neck. In the center portrait, I embellished the hat with a gathered purple bias-cut frill, and adorned the neck of the blouse with a bow comprised of two tacked-down loop stitches, a horizontal straight stitch, and two Japanese ribbon stitches. I trimmed the hat in the portrait at right with loop stitches made with 4mm variegated ribbon and brown bias-cut ribbon feathers. I then added vintage glass beads and buttons as jewelry.

For the borders around the portraits, I created a floral medley of spider web roses, French knots, straight stitch buds, and feather stitches, then twined 7mm lavender organdy ribbon with stitched pearls and glass beads throughout.

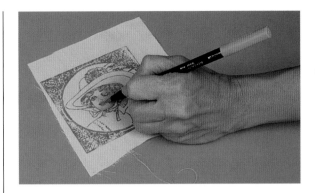

Selected areas of the stamped prints were colored in lightly with fabric markers.

(Right) A detail of the center portrait, and the completed framed project (below).

EMBROIDERED ÉTUI

MATERIALS

Project
Étui kit from Home Arts

Fabrics
1 yard (0.9 m) salmon vintage flower-and-leaf-pattern silk brocade

1 yard (0.9 m) bronze leaf-pattern jacquard silk

Ribbon
1 yard (0.9 m) ¹/₂-inch (1.3-cm) brown bias-cut silk

9 inches (22.9 cm) ¹/₂-inch (1.3-cm) green wire-edge

Thread and Floss
1 spool copper metallic thread

1 spool gold metallic thread

1 skein silver rayon floss

1 skein terracotta rayon floss

Embellishments
20 vintage hexagonal brown glass beads

24 inches (61 cm) gold braided gimp

Green jade rabbit with gold tassel

2 yards (1.8 m) gold cord

Miscellaneous
1 yard (0.9 m) 100-percent wool batting

Fabric glue

E6000 adhesive

In this project, an *étui* (pronounced ay-TWEE), which is a small box or case, is embellished with metallic threads, gathered and ruched flowers, and vintage glass beads. Popular in France during the early 18th century, étuis were used by women to carry personal articles and sewing supplies such as needles, scissors, and thimbles. The étui shown on the opposite page was constructed from a kit available from Home Arts (see the source directory). To assemble the étui, simply follow the kit instructions. While I chose to create a sewing box featuring a pin cushion, the étui can be used as a jewelry box or to hold playing cards and bridge tallies, or can be presented as a gift to an avid collector of unusual boxes. This project required a considerable investment of time, labor, and expense, but the results were well worth the effort.

STITCHING

The lid design was inspired by a piece in my textile collection, an old silk piano cloth that is heavily couched with metal threads. For the lid of the étui, I couched copper thread to the bronze jacquard with gold thread in flower, leaf, and tendril shapes, then filled in the petals and some of the leaves with satin stitches made with two strands of silver and terracotta rayon floss. I ruched brown bias-cut ribbon to make flowers, whose centers I stitched with brown glass beads, which I also stitched into leaf shapes.

I embellished the pin cushion on the inside of the étui with gathered green ribbon flowers, ruched brown bias-cut ribbon, and brown bias-cut Japanese ribbon stitch leaves.

ASSEMBLY

I covered the exterior of the box with the bronze jacquard silk and the interior with the salmon silk brocade. To pad the lid, I used two layers of 100-percent wool batting. I chose a natural batting material because I wanted to create an heirloom; wool batting is frequently used by quilters for its archival qualities. I adhered the fabrics to the cardboard pieces with fabric glue. (Before you use a fabric glue, test it on a small or concealed area to ensure that it will dry to a clear finish and won't stain the fabric.)

To complete the étui, I threaded a gold cord through the pockets at the tops of the segmented sides and glued gold braided gimp (an ornamental flat braid) around the perimeter of the lid. To make the lid pull, I used E6000 to glue a green jade rabbit with a decorative gold tassel to the top.

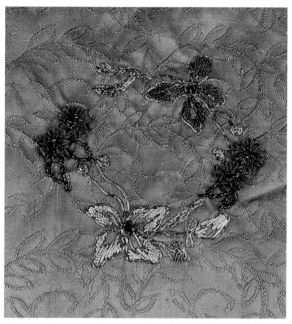

A piece of bronze silk jacquard stitched for the étui lid.

The completed étui, shown closed (above) and open (below).

CHINESE WATERCOLOR

This project proves that inspiration can come from unexpected sources. I adapted the featured image from a watercolor entitled "Paired Swallows and Mandarin Ducks," which was painted by a Chinese artist named Zhou Zhimian during the 1590s. I had seen a color reproduction of the original work in *Masterworks of Ming and Qing Painting from the Forbidden City: A Color Catalogue of Paintings from the Palace Museum in Beijing, China* by Howard Rogers and Sherman E. Lee (Lansdale, Pennsylvania: International Arts Council, 1989). I thought it would complement the intended painting surface beautifully: The color and luminous finish of the gold silk paper evoked the soft ochre tones of the paper on which the original had been rendered.

PENCIL SKETCH AND WATERCOLOR
I began by mounting the paper on a large Q-Snap. Because I knew that the paper would sag when the watercolor washes were applied, I realized I could adjust the tension on the Q-Snap in order to take up the slack. In any event, it would have to be mounted gently because the paper was so fragile. Using my stitching stand for the entire project made the time spent painting and stitching much more comfortable.

Working freehand, I lightly sketched the drawing on the paper with a pencil. Since the silk component of the paper made it impossible to erase any pencil marks without distorting or damaging it, I worked carefully and deliberately, knowing that my sketch would remain visible through the watercolor.

Using a Chinese calligraphy brush for large areas and a liner brush for the details, I laid in light washes of black and burnt umber, then added ultramarine blue mixed with both colors throughout the hills. I let the watercolors dry completely (heat-setting was not required). Leaving the paper mounted on the Q-Snap, I then proceeded to the stitching stage.

STITCHING
I stitched Japanese ribbon stitch leaves in the trees and around the water's edge with the green-and-bronze silk ribbon. To create cherry blossoms, I stitched one-wrap French knots among the branches of the trees with the red-and-pink ribbon, then filled in the remaining blossoms with white ribbon. I then used the floss to stitch one of the Mandarin ducks in shades of orange, rust, and brown.

The completed composition, embellished with stitching.

SILK-APPLIQUÉD BLOUSE

This project embodies many of the stitching and fabric embellishment techniques demonstrated in this book. I purchased a white silk blouse at a thrift shop for only $3.00, but its high quality could be seen in details like silk-covered buttons.

DYEING

I handwashed the blouse in a mild detergent, allowed it to dry, then dyed it in purple. Three dark spots that could not have been seen on the undyed blouse were now visible, so they determined where the elements of the design would be placed—on the front of the blouse between two buttons, on the pocket, and on the right shoulder.

APPLIQUÉ

To create the dominant element, I cut a hand-dyed remnant of silk charmeuse into a variety of leaf shapes and burned their edges. I then laid the silk leaves on the blouse, experimenting with several arrangements and trying to fit them together like puzzle pieces until I was satisfied with each grouping. I lightly dabbed a small amount of craft glue on the back of each leaf to secure it to the blouse, then used a single strand of pink silk thread to appliqué it with small straight stitches.

STITCHING

I gathered 4mm ribbons, then tacked them down with Nymo thread. I stitched Japanese ribbon stitch leaves with 4mm and 7mm hand-dyed green and purple silk ribbons, then added long feather stitch branches with purple metallic filament. On the front of the blouse between the buttons, I stitched three small tubes made from 13mm mauve silk ribbon. As finishing touches, I added clusters and strings of Delica and iridescent glass beads throughout, stitched bugle beads inside the tubes, and used several small amethyst chunk beads to highlight the shoulder design.

Silk charmeuse was cut and burned into leaf shapes, then appliquéd.

The completed blouse.

Details of the shoulder (right), front (below left), and pocket (below right).

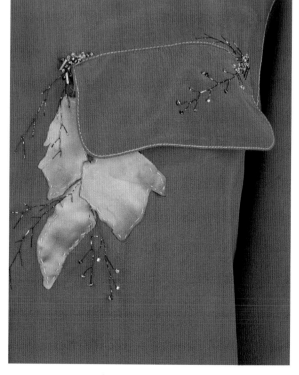

CRAZY-QUILTED DRESS FORM

STITCHES

Lazy daisy

Feather/fly stitch

Straight stitch

Two-ribbon spiral rose

Japanese ribbon stitch

Whip stitch

Stem stitch

Pistil stitch

MATERIALS

Project

Papier-mache dress form

Fabrics

Silk, muslin, and 82-percent rayon/ 18-percent silk velvet

Ribbon

Organdy, ombré, and variegated in a range of widths

Thread

Rayon, silk, and metallic thread in various colors

Dual-duty thread

Nymo beading thread

Embellishments

Gold Delica beads

Vintage metal beads, pearls, and sequins

Green glass bugle beads

Burgundy seed beads

Gold braid in two widths

Red tassle

Miscellaneous

Dylon Cold Water Dye (in "Camellia")

Fiber-Etch Fabric Remover

Paint brush

Fade-away pen

White tacky glue

This project, a miniature dress form covered with various fabrics hand-dyed in the same color, features a foam-stamp print that "etched" into hand-dyed velvet using a craft and sewing product called Fiber-Etch Fabric Remover (available from Silkpaint Corporation, Inc.). This gel, which dissolves all types of plant-based fibers, including cotton, linen, ramie, rayon, and paper, is typically used to create lace cutwork, reverse appliqué, and "windows" (open areas) in painted fabrics. When applied to velvet with a foam stamp, Fiber-Etch dissolves the rayon nap in the shape of the stamp print to reveal the silk base fabric. Note that *only* foam stamps can be used with this product, and that large-scale stamps used to decorate walls seem to work best, as they provide a large surface area for the gel to adhere to. The stamp-etch technique can be used to make either a single print or a lively repeat pattern. Always make a few test prints before stamp-etching a project.

The dress form, which stands 14 inches (35.6 cm) high, is made of papier-mâché and has a hardwood maple base and finial.

DYEING AND STAMP-ETCHING

First, I dyed several remnants of silk, velvet, and polycotton fabric in the same color, then cut them into patch-size pieces. I applied a thin, uniform layer of Fiber-Etch gel to the foam stamp die with a brush, making sure I used enough to leave an obvious print on the back of the velvet. (Because the velvet was so heavy, I applied the gel to the back to ensure that all fibers would be completely saturated.) I stamped the loaded stamp on the back of the velvet, then set the print with a hair dryer. I ironed the print with a dry iron set on the "wool" setting to activate the gel, and when the gel turned brown I rinsed the velvet in water and the treated fibers dropped away from the fabric. The fabric can be allowed to air dry or dried on the "air only" setting for 20 minutes.

A few helpful hints on Fiber-Etch gel: Lighter-weight fabrics may not need as heavy an application of gel, and may not need to be ironed as long as to set it. If you accidently spill any gel on the fabric, simply rinse it while the gel is still damp.

Apply an even layer of Fiber-Etch gel to the foam stamp with a brush.

PIECING AND STITCHING

I created a foundation for piecing the patches together by draping a piece of muslin over the form, pinning the muslin into shape, then removing it from the form. Using a ¹/₄-inch (0.6-cm) seam allowance so that no raw edges would be visible, I basted the patches onto the muslin foundation with dual-duty thread, starting with the stamp-etched velvet patch. I embellished the seams of the patches with crazy quilt and embroidery stitches using metallic and rayon threads and small Japanese ribbon stitches in 4mm silk ribbon. I removed the basting threads, then added some small gold Delica beads among the decorative stitches.

To achieve a vintage look in my designs, I seek out old costume jewelry at antique stores and recycle their components, which often include beautiful old faux pearls and rhinestones. Many of the beads and stones in these older pieces are far superior in quality to what is available today, and thus will give your stitch designs more glitter and style. Combing through my collection, I emphasized the stamp-etched rose print by stitching tiny vintage hexagonal metal beads around its perimeter.

I then sketched two large groupings of flower stitches on two of the patches with a fade-away pen. One arrangement includes three two-ribbon spiral roses made with 4mm red and yellow-orange variegated ribbons. I added two types of leaves—gathered leaves in green ombré ribbon and Japanese ribbon stitch leaves in 7mm green organdy—to complement the design. I completed the grouping with whip stitches in variegated rose ribbon, vintage beige pearls, green glass bugle beads, and a single gold bead. The other floral design features three gathered flowers in red-orange ombré ribbon with gold bead centers, 7mm and 9mm green silk and organdy Japanese ribbon stitch leaves, green silk buttonhole twist stem stitches, and purple metallic thread pistil stitches. Embellishments include vintage starburst sequins, vintage pearls, and burgundy seed beads. As a final touch, I couched ¹/₂-inch (1.3-cm) gold braid around the seams of the velvet patch.

ASSEMBLY

To cover the back of the dress form, I whip stitched a piece of velvet to either side of the pieced composition. I slipped the foundation over the dress form, then trimmed the bottom to leave a ¹/₂-inch (1.3-cm) hem. I glued the hem to the papier-mâché form, then glued 1-inch (2.5-cm) gold braid around the bottom of the form with white tacky glue (a low-temperature glue gun could also be used). I gathered two rows of orange ombré wire-edge ribbon to make a neck ruffle, then glued a piece of the ¹/₂-inch (1.3-cm) gold braid down its center. I completed the form by stitching a red tassle underneath the ruffle over the right shoulder.

(Right) The completed dress form with a stamp-etched rose print, gathered and embroidered flowers, and crazy patch stitches, and a detail of the front of the composition (below).

MIXED-MEDIA WALL HANGING

The design of this piece, which includes dyeing, appliqué, stamping, crazy-quilt stitching, and polymer clay, was inspired by a 1930s children's book in which small, elflike children known as "Twinkies" left their homes—stars in distant galaxies—to visit the Earth. The dimensions of the finished wall hanging are 18 × 24 inches (45.7 × 61 cm).

APPLIQUÉ AND STAMPING

To create the appliqué stars, I recycled several silk ties printed with traditional foulard patterns that I had purchased at a thrift store. I opened the seams, removed the linings, and dyed the ties in Rit dye following the package instructions. Using a cardboard template, I cut four stars from the widest parts of the ties (leaving a 1/4-inch [0.6-cm] seam allowance), then set them aside. To determine the placement of the four appliqués within the composition, I traced the outline of the template on the green rayon fabric with white dressmaker's chalk, then stamped the areas surrounding the outlines with star-shaped sponge and eraser stamps inked with gold Lumiere paint. I cut out a small piece of painter's canvas to make the village, then used fusible webbing to appliqué it to the green fabric. To appliqué the stars, I used appliqué paper and 1/4-inch (0.6-cm) fusible webbing tape.

SKETCHING AND STITCHING

I drew a village on the canvas appliqué with Zig fabric markers. I then outlined all of the appliqués with embroidery and crazy quilt stitches, using two strands of burgundy, navy, and hunter green rayon floss. I stitched small gold Delica beads in some of the windows of the village houses to represent lights.

(Opposite left) These silk ties, which I purchased at a thrift shop, served as the basis for the star appliqués. The developing composition: (Opposite right) The chalk outlines of the appliquéd stars, the appliqué of painter's canvas for the village, and stamp prints made with gold paint, and the appliquéd elements embellished with stitching and the village drawn with fabric markers (right).

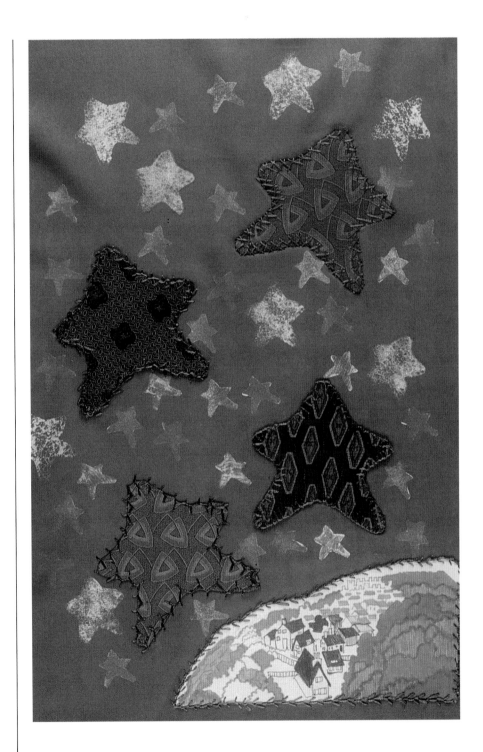

QUILTING AND ASSEMBLY

I applied two layers of wool batting to the back of the fabric, then quilted some of the stamp prints with straight stitches using gold metallic thread, and embellished others with gold Delica and stone beads. I then stitched the backing to the front, and added fabric tabs along the top. Using a Zig opaque gold permanent marker, I printed "Twinkle, twinkle, little star" on the bottom lefthand side of the wall hanging.

I purchased the wooden dowel and finials at a craft store, and had the dowel cut to the width of the wall hanging. I stained both with a light oak stain, let them dry, and sealed them with three coats of spray glaze, letting each coat dry well before applying the next.

TASSELS

I began making the tassels by covering four small wooden cups with ivory and burgundy polymer clay. I kneaded the clay, rolled each color into thin ropes, twisted several ropes of both colors together, then wound them around the wooden cups, leaving the drill holes uncovered. To adhere the clay to the cups, I applied small touches of craft glue with a toothpick and lay the twisted ropes over it. I dabbed a small amount of gold pigment on the clay to impart a lustrous antique finish. I cured the clay in the oven following the package directions, let the cups cool, then finished them with several coats of FolkArt spray glaze (see page 114), letting each dry before applying the next.

To make each tassel, I wrapped a 2- × 4-inch (5- × 10.2-cm) piece of cardboard three colors of rayon thread, sixty times each. I tied and knotted a 6-inch (15.2-cm) piece of thread around one end of the wound thread, clipped open the wound thread at the other end, and removed it from the cardboard. To make the tassel head, I tied another 6-inch (15.2-cm) piece of thread 1 inch (2.5 cm) below the gathered end. I trimmed the ends of the tassel threads to make them even and ironed them so they would lie straight. I applied some craft glue to the head to the tassel, then inserted it into one of the wooden cups. Once I had completed all four tassels, I cut the burgundy cording in half and wrapped each end tightly with tape, applied glue to it, then pushed it into the small drill hole of one of the clay-covered cup. As a finishing touch, I tied two overhand knots in the cords right above the tassel cups.

To complete the wall hanging, I threaded the dowel through the tabs and placed a tasseled cord next to each finial.

To apply the Pearl Ex pigment to the uncured clay, dab a small amount on your index finger and rub it on. You can mix the pigment into the clay before rolling it into ropes, or apply it to the twisted clay ropes after gluing them to the wooden tassel cups.

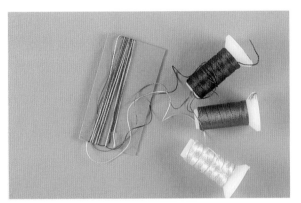

To make the tassels, wrap thread around the cardboard, tie it off at one end, then cut it at the other.

The completed tassels.

The completed wall hanging displayed with tassels and dowel.

ENGLISH GARDEN SCENE

STITCHES
Punch needle
Feather stitch
Japanese ribbon stitch
French knot
Pistil stitch

MATERIALS
Fabrics
1 yard (0.9 m) 25-count ivory linen
1 yard (0.9 m) upholstery-grade moiré
Buckram remnants
Ribbon
Organdy, satin, and silk in various widths and colors
Thread and Yarn
Forest green silk buttonhole twist
Nymo beading thread
Gold wool yarn
Rayon floss in various colors
Embellishments
Gold and green Delica beads
Vintage brown glass beads
Brass bunny charm
Miscellaneous
Water-soluble fabric marker
Q-Snap
Punch needles
PerfectSew fabric stabilizer
Delta Starlite Dye Shimmering Fabric Colors
Polymer clay
Pearl Ex pigments
Black fabric marker
Spray glaze
E6000 adhesive

This project is my favorite because it exemplifies why I wanted to write this book: To show several different media can be easily layered and combined. For me, this project presented two challenges: How to express depth and dimension within a composition by following the basic principles of perspective and by exploiting the characteristics of each medium; and how to create two distinct but complementary designs within the same project. To see this project take shape and finally come to fruition after thinking about it for more than a year was something of a personal triumph. I actually stitched the piece twice, because I hadn't achieved the degree of depth I had originally envisioned on my first try.

INITIAL STITCHING
I mounted the linen on the Q-Snap, then sketched the entire image with a water-soluble fabric marker. (I used a 25-count linen because it is essential to work with a loose-weave fabric when using punch needle.) To convey depth, I began by punching in the grass with the 4mm dark green ribbon, then completed it with 4mm olive ribbon and three strands of olive floss. I stitched the thatched roof with one strand of gold wool to heighten its dimension, then with two strands of gold floss, then finished it with two strands of gold rayon thread. I stitched the wood timbers with two strands of brown floss and the outline of the window with one strand of black rayon floss. I added feather stitch vines and flower stems with green silk buttonhole twist, and Japanese ribbon stitch leaves and flowers (and a few single-wrap French knots) with green, orange, pink, and purple 2mm ribbon. I then stitched some beads throughout the flowers and gold Delica beads in some of the windowpanes to simulate light.

APPLIQUÉ
I cut 32mm green spark organdy into tree shapes and appliquéd them to the background with Nymo thread, building them up in several layers to yield a dark shade of green. In two cases, I stitched trunks and branches with two strands of brown floss before appliquéing the organdy shapes. I then coated the appliqués with PerfectSew to keep the organdy from fraying and to seal its edges. I emphasized the horizon line by stitching a row of green Delica beads beneath the trees.

FABRIC PAINTING AND FINAL STITCHING
I painted the entire fabric ground with a water-thinned wash of Delta Starlite Dye Shimmering Fabric Color in olive green, letting the fabric show through in some areas. I then painted in some clouds with a blue wash.

To complete the stitching, I added Japanese ribbon stitch leaves and flowers with olive green and purple ribbon, straight stitch stems in forest green silk thread, and French knot buds with 2mm hand-dyed coral ribbon.

POLYMER CLAY

I wanted my embellishments to be thick enough to stand out in relief against the stitching, so I rolled out a small amount of each color to an $^1/_8$ inch (0.32 cm) thickness. I used beige for the birdbath, red for the chimney, brown for the wooden door, and gray for the steps. I added details to all of the embellishments with a black textile marker, and applied a mixture of green and bronze Pearl Ex pigments to the birdbath to give it a verdigris finish. I cured the clay pieces according to the manufacturers directions, let them cool, then sprayed each piece with several coats of FolkArt Spray Clearcote High-Shine Brilliant Glaze, letting each coat dry before applying the next. I affixed the clay embellishments (and a gold brass bunny charm) to the fabric ground with E6000 adhesive after the finished piece had been framed.

PICTURE MAT

To heighten the dimensional effect, I made a picture mat out of ivory upholstery-grade moiré, then embroidered it with a variety of flowers. I began by stem stitching the vine with two strands of olive green rayon thread. I then added Japanese ribbon stitch leaves in 13mm and 32mm dark olive green spark organdy. I made two gathered ruffled flowers with two-sided purple-and-lavender satin ribbon and tacked them to small pieces of buckram, and a large gathered flower with 32mm lavender spark organdy, then stitched them all to the mat. I stitched a cluster of three mauve moiré ribbon berries to the top left corner, then added a segmented rose satin ribbon berry to the center of a flower comprised of a circle of 9mm blue organdy Japanese ribbon stitches.

I finished the mat by making two gathered pods out of rose satin ribbon; extending from each pod is a pistil stitch in brown rayon floss with vintage brown glass beads at its tip. The final touches were pistil stitches in olive rayon floss.

The completed English garden and cottage composition with embroidered mat. The piece was framed so that the lavender organdy flower would overlap the frame's edge.

SOURCE DIRECTORY

Listed at right are the manufacturers and wholesale suppliers for many of the materials used in this book. These companies sell their products exclusively to sewing and notions, fabric, needlearts, craft, and hobby retailers, which are a consumer's most dependable sources for silk ribbon embroidery supplies. Your local retailer's knowledgeable personnel can advise you on your purchases, and if you need something they don't have in stock they will usually order it for you. If you can't find a store in your area that carries a particular item or will accept a request for an order, or if you need special assistance, a manufacturer will gladly direct you to the retailer nearest you that carries their products and will try to answer any other questions you might have.

MANUFACTURERS AND WHOLESALE DISTRIBUTORS

SYNTHETIC AND SILK RIBBONS

C. M. Offray & Son
360 Route 24
Chester, New Jersey 07930
(908) 879-4700/FAX (908) 879-8588

Elsie's Exquisiques
208 State Street
St. Joseph, Michigan 49085
(616) 982-0449/FAX (616) 982-0963

Lacis
3163 Adeline Street
Berkeley, California 94703
(510) 843-7178/FAX (510) 843-5018

Mokuba Ribbon
Distributed by Wright's International
P.O. Box 398
West Warren, Massachusetts 01092
(800) 628-9362/FAX (413) 436-9785

Ribbon Connections
969 Industrial Road – Suite E
San Carlos, California 94704
(415) 593-5221/FAX (415) 593-6785

THREADS, FLOSSES, AND YARNS

Alyce Schroth Sampler Recreations
3598 Buttonwood Drive
Doylestown, Pennsylvania 18901
Hand-dyed silk flosses

Bond America
178 Maple Street
Glens Falls, New York 12801
(518) 798-3767/FAX (518) 798-3819
"Multis" variegated threads

Caron Collection
67 Poland Street
Bridgeport, Connecticut 06605
(203) 333-0325
Fibers and threads

It's Polite to Point
1887 Cedar Drive
Severn, Maryland 21144-1005
(800) 688-4424/FAX (410) 551-5989
100-percent Persian needleart wool

DYES, PAINTS, AND RELATED SUPPLIES

Koh-I-Noor
100 North Street
Bloomsbury, New Jersey 08804
(800) 877-3165/FAX (908) 479-4285
Elegance Fabric Dye

Prym-Dritz Corporation
P.O. Box 5028
Spartanburg, South Carolina 29304
Dylon Cold Water Fabric Dye and ribbon embroidery needles

Rupert, Gibbon & Spider
P.O. Box 425
Healdsburg, California 95448
(800) 442-0455/FAX (707) 433-4906
Jacquard Procion MX Fiber-Reactive Dyes, Jacquard Silk Colors, Jacquard Dye-na-Flow, Lumiere Metallic Fabric Paints, Pearl Ex Mica Powdered Pigments, silk and velvet fabrics, Jacquard Wood Products stitchery stands, and ReDuRan hand cleaner

Savior-Faire
P.O. Box 2021
Sausalito, California 94966
(800) 863-9444/FAX (415) 332-3113
Tinfix, Super Tinfix, and Peintex Dyes, squirrel hair brushes, and foam rollers

Silkpaint Corporation, Inc.
18220 Waldron Drive – P.O. Box 18-5R
Waldron, Missouri 64902-0018
(816) 891-7774/FAX (816) 891-7775
H. Dupont Dyes, The AirPen, Fiber-Etch gel, and steaming nets

Things Japanese
9805 N.E. 116th Street
Kirkland, Washington 98034-4248
(206) 821-2287/FAX (206) 821-3554
ColorHue Instant-Set Dyes

George Weil
Reading Arch Road
Redhill, Surrey
England RH1 1HG
01737 778866/FAX 01737 778894
Fabric paints, dyes, related equipment, and silks

MISCELLANEOUS SUPPLIES

American Traditional Stencils
442 First New Hampshire Turnpike
Northwood, New Hampshire 03261
(800) 448-6656/FAX (800) 448-6654
Metal stencils

Bernadine's Needle Art
P.O. Box 41
Arthur, Illinois 61911
(217) 543-2996/FAX (217) 543-2425
Punch needles

Camp Stamp USA
1751 Andrea Avenue
Carlsbad, California 92008
(760) 729-3444/FAX (760) 729-6123
Num Nums rubber stamps

The Crowning Touch, Inc.
2410 Glory "C" Road
Medford, Oregon 97501
(541) 772-8430/FAX (541) 858-9455
Fasturn tool

Elna, Inc.
7642 Washington Avenue South
Eden Prairie, Minnesota 55344
(612) 941-5519/FAX (612) 941-8473
Elna Press Mini Tailor

EK Success Ltd.
611 Industrial Road
Carlstadt, New Jersey 07062
(800) 524-1349/FAX (800) 767-2963
Zig textile markers

Fiskars
7811 West Steward Avenue
Wausau, Wisconsin 54401
(715) 842-2091/FAX (715) 848-5528
Rotary cutters and mats

Home Arts
2101 Fifth Street
Atwater, California 95301
(800) 484-9923, PIN# 2787
Étui kit

Hot Potatoes
209 10th Avenue South – Suite 311
Nashville, Tennessee 37203
(615) 255-4055/FAX (615) 255-4556
Hard red rubber stamps

Kate's Appliqué Paper
270 Fourth Avenue
San Francisco, California 94118
(415) 752-1155/FAX (415) 752-4004
Acid-free appliqué paper

Love To Bead
P.O. Box 8492
Asheville, North Carolina 28814
(704) 252-0274/FAX (704) 254-1486
Delica seed beads and Nymo beading thread

Palmer/Pletsch
P.O. Box 12046
Portland, Oregon 97212
(503) 274-0687/FAX (503) 274-1377
PerfectSew fabric stabilizer

Qualin International, Inc.
749 Monterey Boulevard
San Francisco, California 94127-2221
(415) 333-8500/FAX (415) 282-8789
Silk blanks, silk ribbon, and silk painting supplies

Quilter's Fancy
P.O. Box 457
Cortland, Ohio 44410
(800) 484-7944/FAX (330) 637-3106
Ruching edge

Quilter's Resource
P.O. Box 148850
Chicago, Illinois 60614
(312) 278-5695/FAX (312) 278-1348
Sewing supplies, trims, and kits

RibbonSmyth
P.O. Box 416
Fountainville, Pennsylvania 18923
(215) 249-1258/FAX (215) 249-3628
E-mail: 102515,3570@Compuserve.com
*Vintage kits, Victorian ribbon stamps,
"Ribbon Dyes," and "Stamp and Stitch" kits*

Ruthmarie Originals
4448 Winners Circle
Rocklin, California 95677
(916) 624-6962
*Handmade papers, semiprecious stone beads,
and tassel kits*

Warm Products, Inc.
11610 Woodinville-Redmond Road, #4
Woodinville, Washington 98072
(206) 488-4464/FAX (206) 488-2630
*Warm & Natural wool batting and Steam-A-
Seam fusible webbing*

INDEX